Empowered lives.
Resilient nations.

ASSESSMENT OF DEVELOPMENT RESULTS SOMALIA
EVALUATION OF UNDP CONTRIBUTION

Independent Evaluation Office, October 2016
United Nations Development Programme

REPORTS PUBLISHED UNDER THE ADR SERIES

Afghanistan
Albania
Algeria
Angola
Argentina
Armenia
Bangladesh
Barbados and OECS
Benin
Bhutan
Bosnia and Herzegovina
Botswana
Brazil
Bulgaria
Burkina Faso
Cambodia
Chile
China
Colombia
Croatia
Dominican Republic
Democratic Republic of Congo
Republic of the Congo
Costa Rica
Côte d'Ivoire
Djibouti
Ecuador
Egypt
El Salvador
Ethiopia

Gabon
Georgia
Ghana
Guatemala
Guyana
Honduras
India
Indonesia
Iraq
Jamaica
Jordan
Kenya
Lao PDR
Liberia
Libya
Malawi
Malaysia
Maldives
Mauritania
Moldova
Mongolia
Montenegro
Morocco
Mozambique
Nepal
Nicaragua
Niger
Nigeria
Pacific Islands
Papua New Guinea

Paraguay
Peru
The Philippines
Rwanda
Sao Tome and Principe
Senegal
Serbia
Seychelles
Sierra Leone
Somalia
Sri Lanka
Sudan
Syrian Arab Republic
Tajikistan
Tanzania
Thailand
Timor-Leste
Tunisia
Turkey
Uganda
Ukraine
United Arab Emirates
United Republic of Tanzania
Uruguay
Uzbekistan
Viet Nam
Yemen
Zambia
Zimbabwe

ASSESSMENT OF DEVELOPMENT RESULTS: SOMALIA

DISCLAIMER

Carried out between mid-2014 and mid-2015, the UNDP Assessment of Development Results (ADR) in Somalia took into consideration the developments in the country from January 2011 to June 2015. The Independent Evaluation Office (IEO), by way of advice from the country office and Regional Bureau for Arab States, is cognizant of the progress made by Somalia in consolidating its Peacebuilding and State-building Goals under Vision 2016 and the Somali Compact since the completion of the ADR. It is the view of the country office and the Regional Bureau that some of the conclusions and recommendations of this report, particularly regarding capacity-building, are not fully applicable to the current UNDP programme in Somalia.

The IEO did not have the opportunity to verify or assess the recent (since June 2015) contributions of UNDP, but understands that UNDP continued to support the Federal Government of Somalia in achieving its goals. UNDP refocused its portfolio and programmatic delivery away from three separate entities (Puntland, Somaliland and South Central) to supporting a new federal Somalia consisting possibly of six or seven member states, including a 'special arrangement' for Somaliland. UNDP Somalia expanded its programmatic and operational footprint with the deployment of national staff to new locations in emerging state capitals, with the objective of strengthening institutional capacity. UNDP contributed to the establishment of the aid architecture for the Somali Compact and coordinated donor support for capacity development of the new Aid Coordination Unit, which serves as the secretariat to the Somalia Development and Reconstruction Facility.

In partnership with the United Nations Assistance Mission in Somalia (UNSOM), UNDP supported nationwide consultations to agree on a new electoral model, leading to its endorsement via Presidential decree in May 2016. UNDP contributed to the establishment of the National Independent Electoral Commission in early July 2015, with capacity-building assistance to this nascent institution. UNDP also supported the adoption of state constitutions, state presidential elections and the formation of state ministries and assemblies. In addition, UNDP supported the roll-out of the constitutional review process at the state and federal levels and provided technical expertise to the Parliament and local assemblies.

Since 2015, a new capacity development project has replaced the Somalia Institutional Development Project (SIDP). The new project, developed after extensive consultation with all stakeholders including the World Bank, has built on the SIDP experience and benefited from previous evaluation findings. As a result, the public financial management component no longer lies with UNDP. The project continues to provide ad hoc consultancy support but the relationship is based on concrete deliverables and their implementation. UNDP has also been a key partner to the Ministry of Planning and International Cooperation in taking forward the National Development Plan process, through the deployment of specialized expertise embedded in the Ministry, in addition to the longer-term support to strengthen its planning, monitoring and evaluation and statistical capacities.

UNDP provided technical assistance for the preparation of the National Action Plan to Combat Desertification and the intended nationally determined contributions report on climate change ahead of Somalia's participation in the United Nations Climate Change Conference in Paris in December 2015. UNDP has repositioned its environment portfolio towards addressing the root causes of environmental degradation such as unsustainable charcoal production, desertification and drought. In December 2015, UNDP, in partnership with the Ministry of Energy and the International Renewable Energy Agency, completed the 'Renewable Energy Readiness' report, which will provide the platform to scale up renewable energy programming, particularly solar energy, across the country. Throughout 2015, UNDP also supported the establishment of an early warning centre in Somaliland equipped with technical resources for data collection, analysis and monitoring of trends leading to drought and flooding. A similar centre will be established in Puntland in 2016.

ACKNOWLEDGEMENTS

The UNDP Independent Evaluation Office (IEO) would like to thank all who contributed to this evaluation. The evaluation team was led and managed by Michael Reynolds. Other team members included Olivier Cossee (poverty reduction and environment team leader); Ximena Rios (management and operations team leader); and Grace Okonji (gender mainstreaming and women's empowerment team leader). Midway through the evaluation, Deqa Ibrahim Musa took over from Michael Reynolds as evaluation manager. She updated and finalized the report.

We extend our appreciation to a wide range of stakeholders who generously shared their time and ideas throughout the evaluation process. We thank the Federal Government of Somalia, in particular the Permanent Secretary, Ministry of National Planning and International Cooperation, the Honourable Abdi Dirshe. We would also like to thank the staff of UNDP Somalia, especially George Conway (Country Director), David Akopyan (Deputy Country Director, Programmes) and Bushra Hassan (Monitoring and Evaluation Specialist). We also thank the staff of the UNDP Regional Bureau for Arab States (in particular, Sophie De Caen, Celine Moyroud and Esteban Olhagaray) for their constructive engagement. We are grateful to representatives of the United Nations Country Team in Somalia, donor countries and institutions, civil society and the private sector for generously contributing their time, information and insight to the evaluation.

As part of the quality assurance arrangements, the IEO invited Daniel Weiner, Vice President for Global Affairs, University of Connecticut, and member of the IEO Evaluation Advisory Panel, to serve as an independent external reviewer to assess the quality of the report. We are grateful for his contribution.

We extend out thanks to Katuni Consult, which was contracted by IEO to undertake project-level data collection in Somalia in areas outside those visited by the evaluation team.

The quality enhancement and administrative support provided by our colleagues at the IEO was vital to the evaluation. Vijayalakshmi Vadivelu participated in the internal peer review of the draft report. Michael Craft and Yunzhong Cheng provided research support. Sonam Choetsho and Michelle Sy provided logistical and administrative support. Sasha Jahic managed the production of the report.

FOREWORD

I am pleased to present the Assessment of Development Results (ADR) in Somalia. The UNDP Independent Evaluation Office conducted the ADR between 2014 and 2015. It is the second ADR conducted in Somalia and covers the period January 2011 through June 2015.

In 2012, Somalia witnessed political transition with the adoption of a Provisional Constitution and election of a new Parliament and President. The new President outlined a policy framework for the reconstruction of the country in his 'Six Pillar Policy', prioritizing functioning institutions, economic recovery, peacebuilding, service delivery, international relations and national reconciliation. Supported by the international community through the Somali Compact framework, the Federal Government of Somalia has been making progress on these priorities.

UNDP has been supporting Somali authorities in policy advice and capacity development for poverty reduction, good governance, peacebuilding, gender equality and women's empowerment. The ADR found that the effectiveness and results of this work vary. Work on local governance, peacebuilding, gender mainstreaming and fighting HIV and AIDS generally has made important contributions in these areas, although coverage remains limited. On the other hand, UNDP has been less effective in its work on poverty reduction and capacity development. The ADR recognizes the challenging political and institutional set-up and the huge development needs of Somalia. This report includes a set of recommendations for UNDP to consider during its next country programme, likely to begin in 2018. UNDP management has indicated actions taken since the completion of the ADR in response to the recommendations as well as future actions.

I would like to thank the Federal Government of Somalia and other stakeholders for their support throughout the evaluation process. I hope this report will be of use to UNDP, the Federal Government of Somalia and other development partners in prompting discussions on how UNDP may be best positioned to support Somalia as it undergoes another political transition at the end of 2016.

Indran A. Naidoo
Director
Independent Evaluation Office

TABLE OF CONTENTS

ACRONYMS AND ABBREVIATIONS

ADR	Assessment of Development Results
AEM	Associate Evaluation Manager
AMISOM	African Union Military Observer Mission in Somalia
ART	antiretroviral treatment
BDP	UNDP Bureau for Development Policy
BCPR	UNDP Bureau for Crisis Prevention and Recovery
CPAP	country programme action plan
CPD	country programme document
CSO	civil society organization
DANIDA	Danish International Development Agency
DFID	United Kingdom Department for International Development
DPKO	United Nations Department of Peacekeeping Operations
EM	Evaluation Manager
EU	European Union
FAO	Food and Agricultural Organization of the United Nations
FGM/C	female genital mutilation/cutting
GS	Gender Specialist
HACT	harmonized approach to cash transfers
ICT	information and communication technology
IEO	Independent Evaluation Office
IGAD	Intergovernmental Authority on Development
ILO	International Labour Organization
ISF	Integrated Strategic Framework
JCU	Joint Constitution Unit
M&E	monitoring and evaluation
MP	Member of Parliament
MPI	Multidimensional Poverty Index
MPTF	Multi-Partner Trust Fund for Somalia
NORAD	Norwegian Agency for International Development
NDP	National Development Plan
NGO	non-governmental organization
OCHA	United Nations Office for the Coordination of Humanitarian Affairs
ODA	official development assistance
OS	Operations Specialist
PPU	Project and Planning Unit

PSGs	Peacebuilding and State-building Goals
RBAS	UNDP Regional Bureau for Arab States
RDP	Somali Reconstruction and Development Programme
ROAR	results-oriented annual report
SIDP	Somalia Institutional Development Project
SDRF	Somalia Development and Reconstruction Facility
SWALIM	Somalia Water and Land Information Management
ToR	terms of reference
UNAIDS	Joint United Nations Programme on HIV/AIDS
UNCDF	United Nations Capital Development Fund
UNCT	United Nations Country Team
UNDP	United Nations Development Programme
UNEP	United Nations Environment Programme
UNFPA	United Nations Population Fund
UN-Habitat	United Nations Human Settlements Programme
UNHCR	Office of the United Nations High Commissioner for Refugees
UNICEF	United Nations Children's Fund
UNPOS	United Nations Political Office for Somalia
UNSAS	United Nations Somalia Assistance Strategy
UNSOA	United Nations Support Office for AMISOM
UNSOM	United Nations Assistance Mission in Somalia
UN SWAP	United Nations System-wide Action Plan on Gender Equality and the Empowerment of Women
UN-Women	United Nations Entity for Gender Equality and the Empowerment of Women
USAID	United States Agency for International Development
WFP	World Food Programme

EXECUTIVE SUMMARY

The Independent Evaluation Office (IEO) of the United Nations Development Programme (UNDP) conducted an evaluation in Somalia during 2014 and 2015. This Assessment of Development Results (ADR) primarily covers UNDP initiatives undertaken under the current country programme since 2011 through June 2015. The ADR aims to capture and demonstrate evaluative evidence of the contributions of UNDP to development results in Somalia. The ADR findings are expected to inform the next UNDP country programme. The primary users of the ADR are the UNDP country office and Regional Bureau for Arab States (RBAS).

The evaluation has two main components: (a) the analysis of the UNDP contribution to development results, specifically against the outcomes contained in the country programme document (CPD); and (b) the analysis of the strategy UNDP has adopted to enhance its contribution to development results in Somalia. The unit of analysis for the evaluation is the country programme outcome as detailed in the CPD.

The evaluation used data from primary and secondary sources, including a desk review of documentation and information and interviews with key informants, including government representatives, civil society organizations, private sector representatives, United Nations agencies, multilateral organizations, bilateral donors and beneficiaries of the programme. The evaluation used a process of triangulation of information collected from different sources and methods to ensure that the data are valid.

The ADR was conducted in consultation with the UNDP Somalia country office, RBAS and the Federal Government of Somalia. Programme country Governments normally review ADR reports and participate in a stakeholder workshop along with other development partners to discuss the ADR findings and recommendations. A video teleconference was organized in June 2016 with the Federal Government, UNDP Somalia and IEO stakeholders to validate the evaluation conclusions and recommendations. For security and logistical reasons, the IEO decided not to hold a physical stakeholder workshop in Somalia at the end of the evaluation process.

KEY FINDINGS

EFFECTIVENESS OF THE UNDP CONTRIBUTION

Due to the absence of a strong monitoring and evaluation (M&E) system, the effectiveness of the results of UNDP work can only be assessed based on limited information. Under the poverty reduction and environment programme, the overall picture is one of interesting and useful work, but undertaken at too small a scale to respond to actual needs. Given the size of the country, the national ambition of the programme, the top-heaviness of the programme cost structure, the high operational costs in Somalia and modest success so far in attracting funding, interventions under this outcome amount to a collection of small, 'on-off' injections of assistance in various locales, which are neither cumulative nor transformative. Under the governance outcome, the level of UNDP effectiveness varies across the programme components. The joint programme on local governance has made a very important contribution to local governance in the area within which it works and potentially beyond. The interventions appear to be very effective and exhibit great promise for further contribution to Somalia's development goals in the future. In contrast, a recent evaluation, on which this ADR builds, assessed the UNDP interventions under the Somalia Institutional Development Project (SIDP) as leading to capacity substitution rather than capacity development. The drafting of the

Provisional Constitution also occurred under the auspices of UNDP with mixed results: the resulting document, while containing many ambiguities and lacking broad stakeholder consultation, is a major achievement. UNDP interventions addressing peacebuilding and security have made a contribution, although it is impossible to assess its full extent without adequate data. On gender mainstreaming, UNDP has been effective in promoting more equal representation and participation of men with women as decision makers and enhancing the quality of women's participation, e.g., building the capacity of women themselves and women's organizations and networks. Efforts aimed at preventing sexual and gender-based violence and helping women to access legal protection have also been effective in contribution to the result area. However, as in other outcome areas, the small size and scope of these initiatives often limited their perceived relevance as being severely inadequate given the enormity of the issue. Finally, UNDP generally has been effective in its work and has made an important contribution to national efforts to fight HIV and AIDS. At the level of policy and coordination, where UNDP has focused on the National AIDS Commissions, there is lack of understanding of the roles played by the Commissions (strengthening and coordinating a multisectoral response) and by the three Ministries of Health (addressing all medical components of the HIV response) which has led to tensions between the commissions and the ministries.

RELEVANCE OF THE
UNDP CONTRIBUTION

RELEVANCE OF THE UNDP CONTRIBUTION

UNDP interventions implemented in Somalia under the poverty reduction and environment programme, including work on private sector development, youth training, income generation and job creation, were generally found to be relevant but quite small in size compared to the overall needs. The relevance of the components under inclusive and accountable governance has also been generally strong. The SIDP is an exception. The recent evaluation of SIDP noted that the biggest challenge for the project was that it was totally supply-driven and that there were limited consultations with the user line ministries before design. The evaluation found the work under peacebuilding and security to be relevant as it is directly aligned with national priorities set out in the Federal Government's Six Pillar Policy as well as with the Somali Compact. In terms of gender, the evaluation found the dual-track approach of the UNDP gender equality and women's empowerment programme was relevant and responded directly to the acute and important needs of Somali women and men, tackling some of the most recurrent aspects of discrimination against women and girls, in particular sexual and gender-based violence, access to legal rights, inequalities in representation and participation in decision-making. Finally, UNDP work on HIV and AIDS, including on developing the basic infrastructure and policy frameworks and on awareness-raising, was found to be relevant in terms of the context and the UNDP mandate within the Joint United Nations Programme on HIV/AIDS (UNAIDS) division of labour among United Nations agencies.

EFFICIENCY OF THE UNDP CONTRIBUTION

The successful mainstreaming by UNDP of cross-cutting programme components such as gender and HIV and AIDS into other interventions, including the joint programme on local governance and the access to justice project, enhances programme synergies and improves the potential for both effectiveness and efficiency. However, the complex structure of the Somalia country office, with offices across the five operational environments within which it works, creates extra challenges for effective and efficient management of the UNDP programme. The sub-offices/area offices are the engines of delivery, particularly in the north where security conditions allow for smoother programme implementation, but they are located at the periphery of the UNDP structure in Somalia and have difficulty solving key administrative issues such as premise contract management. Project implementation and supervision clearly face challenges in a conflict environment or even in the transitional context of Somaliland. Shortfalls were seen in annual programme expenditure targets. Except in 2012 (83 per cent), the overall annual programme implementation rates were lower than the corporate threshold of 80 per cent. The New Deal Compact is very process-oriented, and has generated much talk and expectations, but no new funding was received until mid-2015. This contributed to low efficiency for the first year of the Compact because the level of activity was not as high as envisaged. Implementing partners also reported delays in signing letters of agreement and funds release, although UNDP management has taken steps to address these issues.

SUSTAINABILITY OF THE UNDP CONTRIBUTION

Sustainability is a serious challenge for most of the projects implemented by UNDP. Security is of course a significant issue in most of the country, in addition to a general lack of capacities, including government financial capacities, implying low prospects for sustainability in many of the reviewed projects under the livelihoods outcome. Capacity development and vocational/youth training interventions were fragmented and almost systematically composed of short training sessions and workshops, which are not necessarily sustainable. There is a need to invest in institutions, e.g., to use existing universities and other training centres rather than provide short-term training directly to beneficiaries. Similarly, the engagement on microfinance seems to be inconsistent. The only cases where the ADR team perceived a sense of strong local ownership and therefore a good prospect for sustainability was when the livelihoods interventions were implemented through local governments, e.g., within a partnership within the joint programme on local governance. In the area of access to justice, while there is a limit as to how long UNDP and its donor partners will be able to fund this work, the results are likely to be sustainable. Better use of national institutions such the University of Hargeisa to anchor the legal aid initiative enhances the likelihood of sustainability. Similarly, strong national ownership in the joint programme on local governance means that the results are likely to be sustainable and the use of programme approaches by the Government to expand the scheme is further evidence that the scheme has been institutionalized in that region. In contrast, the internships funded through SIDP are less likely to be sustainable. The majority of SIDP deliverables were focused on capacity substitution, which severely reduces the likelihood of sustainability of results. In the peacebuilding and security outcome, sustainability also remains a challenge. There is some concern over the sustainability of UNDP support to civilian police, especially with respect to stipends. Financial sustainability also appears to be major concern for the community security projects. In the area of gender, elements of sustainability exist but the issue of an exit strategy must be discussed within the context of fragility and the need for a long-term perspective in a context where institutions are still being built and institutional capacity is widely lacking. But the assessment of the gender-specific interventions is more positive for sustainability. Finally, in the HIV and AIDS programme, inadequate institutional and individual capacity development, going beyond training and funding, were noted as constraints to sustainability.

THE STRATEGIC POSITIONING OF UNDP SOMALIA

UNDP has made efforts to remain relevant to national development priorities through the alignment with larger frameworks, most recently the New Deal. This approach, while pragmatic, has required UNDP to make several adjustments to its country programme since it was designed in late 2009 and early 2010, including most recently with the New Deal. The main comparative strength of UNDP lies in its long presence in the country, which is supposed to be reinforced by setting up offices in Mogadishu. UNDP is operating in the context of limited resources and a changing resource mobilization environment. Its local presence in Mogadishu, Garowe and Hargeisa, as costly as it is, allows UNDP to play an intermediary role between donors and national authorities. This strategic position is common in conflict-affected countries, but in Somalia it is resented by both donors and the Government. Donors perceived UNDP neither as a strong intellectual leader nor as a strong, dependable operational channel for programme delivery. This perception is slowly changing and some donors have acknowledged efforts by new senior management to be more transparent and open. All partners appear unhappy about one main issue, the inability to show results. UNDP is undertaking a lot of activities but the results (changes to people's lives or to institutions) are often unclear. This issue goes beyond third-party monitoring of implementation and outputs (fiscal accountability) and concerns the actual outcomes of the work, i.e., to answer the questions of what works, why has it worked, for whom did it work and in what contexts would it work again? Of course, the nature of UNDP interventions means that they often address issues that are inherently long-term in nature and it is often difficult to see results in a few years (e.g., you can easily train and equip police but it can take years for attitudes to change). The context in which UNDP is working has been in continuous flux with repeated turnover of staff.

CONCLUSIONS

Conclusion 1. In Somalia, both the United Nations as a whole and UNDP come under a lot of criticism based largely on the failures of the peacekeeping missions of the 1990s but also on more recent performance, including the work of UNDP in the governance sector (deemed by many internal and external observers to be political, externally driven and too ambitious).[1] This backdrop, combined with Somalia's peculiarly challenging programming environment, makes it even more important to qualify the performance of UNDP in the given context. The ADR finds that UNDP made important contributions to Somalia's development efforts.

Conclusion 2. While the programme and its components generally have been relevant to Somalia's development needs, there has been much greater emphasis on contributing to development, peace and security through addressing governance issues, as opposed to making a contribution through strengthening livelihoods. If UNDP Somalia is to make a meaningful contribution to the organization's corporate vision[2] of eradicating extreme poverty and significantly reducing inequality and exclusion in Somalia, then greater investment is required to strengthen livelihoods.

Conclusion 3. UNDP faces the challenge of remaining relevant across different operating environments (Federal Government, existing and emerging member states and Somaliland) while working through a single country programme. There is a trade-off between the practical reality of adapting to different environments and the need for programme coherence, yet while it is unnecessary to implement every programme component across all regions, there are areas where by doing so, UNDP has helped to bring about coherence across the country.

Conclusion 4. Both the ADR and previous evaluations have found that the UNDP contribution to strengthening national capacities has been less than expected. While sufficient analysis is required to account for the low base from which interventions started, new joint initiatives aimed at broad capacity development in the public sector should also recognize past failures and undertake analysis of context-specific constraints and opportunities.

---

1   See for example: Menkhaus, K, 'A Country in Peril, a Policy Nightmare', ENOUGH Strategy Paper, September 2008; Hashi, A, 'Somalia's Vision 2016: Reality Check and the Road Ahead', The Heritage Institute for Policy Studies, May 2015; Mosley, J, 'Somalia's Federal Future: Layered Agendas, Risks and Opportunities', Chatham House, Royal Institute for International Affairs, September 2015.

2   UNDP Strategic Plan, 2014-2017.

Conclusion 5. UNDP management and staff are committed and receptive to the UNDP gender equality and women's empowerment strategy and the country office has a gender mainstreaming architecture in place. While this is important, UNDP will deliver few gender results if it does not move away from 'soft' support (gender policy, advocacy, lobbying) and coverage of the number of trainees to women's economic empowerment in terms of technical and business skills.

Conclusion 6. Monitoring and reporting of results by UNDP tend to emphasize inputs and immediate outputs with less emphasis on intermediate outcome results. This can be linked to several factors: the broad framework of UNDP support which has to be responsive to Governments; the intangible and difficult-to-measure nature of UNDP support, e.g., strengthening governance systems, capacity development and policy advice; and insufficient institutional capacity (human resources, tools and skills). The corollary for UNDP is the inability to demonstrate its contribution to development results which in turn has consequences for forging effective partnerships and mobilizing resources.

RECOMMENDATIONS

Recommendation 1: Recognizing the complexity and fluidity of the Somali context, the ADR recommends that UNDP Somalia, in developing its new country programme, should continue to pursue an adaptive planning and management approach.

Management response: UNDP Somalia agrees with this recommendation. UNDP has maintained its flexibility in the Somali context by: (a) aligning its programmes to the New Deal priorities and the Compact's Peacebuilding and State-building Goals and by designing and aligning new programmes under the Compact aid architecture; (b) expanding its portfolio specifically to support key political priorities, including electoral support, review of the Constitution and support to newly emerging federal member states, focusing on both the short-term political deliverables and on building institutional

capacity for longer-term democratic development in Somalia; (c) expanding its institutional support to governance institutions such as parliaments in the newly emerging federal member states; and (d) developing a comprehensive youth employment strategy and joint programme to support the long-term employability of Somali youth through strengthening of value chains in key growth sectors, and rolling out new programming to support climate change resilience at community level.

UNDP Somalia is currently supporting the Federal Government in preparing its first National Development Plan (NDP) in more than two decades, in order to focus future development interventions on poverty reduction and address the root causes of vulnerability that underlie the volatile humanitarian context, while continuing to maintain an integrated focus on the intersection between politics, security and development. UNDP will develop its next country programme in alignment with the NDP. The future country programme will reiterate the need for flexibility with regard to immediate priorities while maintaining a commitment to longer-term development objectives and the Sustainable Development Goals.

Recommendation 2: UNDP Somalia should recalibrate the profile of the poverty reduction and environment programme if it is to meet the immediate and long-term needs of the vulnerable population.

Management response: The country office is in broad agreement with the recommendation. The country office's programmatic portfolio on poverty reduction and resilience has been expanding rapidly. Key new projects include the Joint Programme on Youth Employment Somalia (2015–2018), with the United Nations Human Settlements Programme (UN-Habitat), the International Labour Organization (ILO) and the Food and Agricultural Organization of the United Nations (FAO); the Joint Programme for Sustainable Charcoal Reduction and Alternative Livelihoods, with FAO and the United Nations Environment Programme (UNEP); and the Enhancing Climate Resilience of the Vulnerable Communities and Ecosystems in Somalia (2015–

2018) project, funded by the Global Environment Facility. The country office is also developing a new joint programme on durable solutions to displacement in Somalia, with UN-Habitat and the Office of the United Nations High Commissioner for Refugees (UNHCR), as well as new initiatives related to renewable energy, climate-smart approaches to rural development and local economic development.

However, the country office recognizes the need for a forward-looking review of the poverty reduction and environment programme with a focus on longer-term poverty reduction, including shifting from short-term employment to longer-term employment at scale, particularly for youth and women, that will drive economic growth and support overall stability. The new NDP will provide UNDP a key opportunity to reposition its work – and engagement with the Government and donor partners – in favour of a greater focus on poverty reduction, and a strategic review as suggested would assist in this respect.

The comments on regular resources are well noted. UNDP regular resources have played a critical role in initiating new programmes and in bridging gaps when donor funding is sometimes unpredictable. A flexible approach to TRAC allocations is therefore necessary.

Recommendation 3: There is a need to review the country programme's current approach to capacity development and to develop a conceptual framework for more effective and sustainable capacity development across the board.

Management response: The country office is in broad agreement with the recommendation. The ADR findings concerning the often limited impact of capacity development efforts led to the development of a new capacity development programme during 2014 and early 2015. The programme consisted of two main projects – strengthening institutional performance, working on the federal level and in Puntland, and the state formation project, working in the emerging states – both of which became operational during 2015. These are in addition to longstanding support to district governments through the joint programme on local governance,

which is now being expanded to new districts in the south of the country.

Improvements in the country office's overall capacity development approach are taking place on three levels:

- **Focusing capacity development towards core government functions**, *including: planning, monitoring, evaluation and statistics; organizational structures and functional arrangements on vertical and horizontal levels; internal and external coordination mechanisms; civil service management, with a strong focus on human resources management; administrative management (financial, personnel, office systems, etc.); policy and strategy development (systemic improvements); and gender mainstreaming in selected key areas;*

- **Focusing capacity development support on the internal capacities of supporting institutions**, *in line with the overall UNDP approach towards capacity development, with its focus on organizational development, and directly linked to the harmonized approach to cash transfers capacity assessments, as well as functional reviews undertaken. The support provided to government institutions focuses on strengthening internal systems of governance and the individual capacities of staff members to discharge their functions; organizational reforms; regulatory development; designing terms of reference; and classic training of institutional staff;*

- **Stimulating consistency in the approach to capacity development throughout the country programme**. *While specific capacity development projects are being delivered at federal, state and district levels, as noted above, capacity development is an important and cross-cutting element of all UNDP-supported projects. Steps have been taken to further harmonize the capacity development approach and stimulate a higher level of coherence in the country programme. This element, however, does require more attention, which also will be taken forward through the formulation of the new country programme, which is likely to occur towards the end of 2016, bringing the overall programme structure in* *line with the expectations to be expressed in the forthcoming NDP.*

Recommendation 4: UNDP should prioritize substantive gender mainstreaming in the next country programme

Management response: UNDP Somalia agrees with this recommendation. The 2011-2016 country programme had a dedicated gender-specific outcome and provided a framework to implement the corporate mandate of gender mainstreaming across all the country programme outcomes. The country office has made efforts and progress in consolidating past gains, building on lessons learned and drawing inspiration from organizational commitments to gender equality and women's empowerment, as reflected in the Gender Equity Seal 'High Silver' award which the country office received in 2015. Recommendations from the Gender Equality Seal process are being implemented in order to progress towards a target of 'Gold'. Together with other members of the United Nations Country Team, the country office has also supported the representation of gender in the Compact processes, including two side events on women and gender equity issues at the High-Level Partnership Forums in 2015 and 2016. To attain even further results in terms of gender mainstreaming, the country office will focus on the following:

a) *Mainstreaming gender equality and women's empowerment into the next country programme;*

b) *Continued delivery of specific initiatives to advance gender equality and women's empowerment, including on women's political participation, the gender dimension of the NDP and Sustainable Development Goal 5;*

c) *Building and strengthening strategic partnerships to increase the impact of effort towards gender equality and women's empowerment, as recommended by the ADR;*

d) *Improving gender-responsive planning, monitoring, reporting and evaluation.*

Recommendation 5: UNDP should increase investments to enhance internal monitoring and reporting capacities. It is encouraging that UNDP has already initiated alternative institutional arrangements to strengthen results-based monitoring and reporting, such as third-party monitoring in 2015. Capacities of implementing partners to monitor their work during implementation and ex-post should also be assessed and strengthened as part of broader capacity development efforts.

Management response: UNDP Somalia agrees with this recommendation. The country office has strengthened internal monitoring and reporting through a number of means, including increasing the number of national M&E staff in projects and in the Programme and Planning Unit. The third-party monitoring arrangements in place not only verify numbers or activities, but also seek more output- and outcome-related results, including beneficiary satisfaction and project effectiveness. All project documents, annual workplans and partnership agreements are reviewed by the M&E team prior to approval. Similarly, all implementation arrangements (letters of agreement, grants, etc.) are scrutinized through the Local Project Appraisal Committee, to ensure that proper capacity assessment and appropriate risk mitigation measures have been put in place. The letters of agreement and grant agreements also contain requirements for improved partner reporting, third-party monitoring as commissioned by UNDP and provision of beneficiary contacts in order to conduct follow-up verification. The office has revised its reporting templates with a focus on evidence-based reporting and inclusion of monitoring and oversight activities.

In 2016, the country office will continue to develop these arrangements. Work is ongoing to deepen capacity development for national counterparts, specifically in the areas of results-based management and reporting. This includes specific support, for instance to the new M&E team at the Ministry of Planning and International Cooperation on results-based management and monitoring of the Sustainable Development Goals, and on the preparation of the monitoring framework for the new NDP. The country office will continue these efforts through devising a feedback mechanism for senior manage-

ment on monitoring findings and follow-up actions; expanded capacity development for national partners on results-based management and reporting; establishment of a country office M&E working group for national staff; tracking the frequency of monitoring visits undertaken by project and programme staff; and using social media to inform stakeholders of third-party monitoring findings.

INTRODUCTION

The Independent Evaluation Office (IEO) of the United Nations Development Program (UNDP) conducts country evaluations called assessments of development results (ADRs) to capture and demonstrate evaluative evidence of the UNDP contributions to development results at the country level. ADRs are independent evaluations carried out within the overall provisions contained in the UNDP evaluation policy.[3] The IEO is independent of UNDP management and is headed by a Director who reports to the UNDP Executive Board. The purpose of an ADR is to:

- support the development of the next UNDP country programme;

- support greater UNDP accountability to national stakeholders and partners in the programme country;

- strengthen the accountability of UNDP to the Executive Board.

1.1 SCOPE OF THE EVALUATION

The first ADR for Somalia was conducted in 2010 and covered the period 2005-2010. This second ADR was conducted during 2014-2015 and covers the period 2011 to June 2015. It aimed to contribute to the realignment of the ongoing country programme (2011-2015)[4] and the associated gender strategy to ensure consistency with:

- the Somali Compact endorsed at the Conference on A New Deal for Somalia, held in Brussels in September 2013;

- the United Nations Integrated Strategic Framework (2014-2016) that sets out how the United Nations system will support the achievement of the priorities contained in the Somali Compact;

- the UNDP Strategic Plan, 2014-2017 and associated gender equality strategy, 2014-2017.[5]

The ADR also aimed to contribute to the preparation of a new set of programmes due to start in 2015.[6]

The ADR assessed the UNDP contribution to national efforts aimed at addressing development challenges and provide conclusions on the overall performance of UNDP. It assessed key results – anticipated and unanticipated, positive and negative – and covered UNDP assistance funded from both regular and other resources. The evaluation also examined the contribution of the country office gender strategy (2012-2015), which is aligned to the country programme document (CPD), to achieving gender results within UNDP development support to Somalia. Based on the findings from the assessment of past per-

---

3   See UNDP Evaluation Policy: www.undp.org/eo/documents/Evaluation-Policy.pdf. The ADR will also be conducted in adherence to the norms and the standards and the ethical Code of Conduct established by the United Nations Evaluation Group (www.uneval.org).

4   In September 2016, the country office will submit a request to extend the country programme until 2017.

5   The UNDP gender strategy, 2014-2017 provides detailed guidance for UNDP business units on how to mainstream gender perspectives as they operationalize all aspects of the UNDP Strategic Plan, 2014-2017. This includes identifying strategic entry points for advancing gender equality and women's empowerment in all seven outcome areas of the Strategic Plan.

6   The ADR team provided direct feedback to management in August and November 2014 as the report was not prepared in time (see section 1.4).

formance, the evaluation looked ahead to examine how UNDP can improve its development contribution. Special efforts were made to look at operational and management issues and how they have affected this contribution.

1.2 METHODOLOGY

The evaluation has two main components; (a) the analysis of the UNDP contribution to development results (specifically, against the outcomes contained in the CPD); and (b) the analysis of the strategy UNDP has adopted to enhance its contribution to development results in Somalia. For each component, the ADR will present its findings and assessment according to the set criteria provided below. Further elaboration of the criteria will be found in the *ADR Manual 2011*.

- **UNDP contribution by thematic/programmatic areas.** Analysis will be made of the contribution of UNDP to Somalia's development results through its programme activities. The analysis will be presented by outcome areas and according to the following criteria:

  - **Relevance** of UNDP projects and outcomes to the country's needs and national priorities;

  - **Effectiveness** of UNDP interventions in terms of contributing to the programme outcomes;

  - **Efficiency** of UNDP interventions in terms of use of human and financial resources;

  - **Sustainability** of the results to which UNDP contributed.

- **UNDP contribution through its strategic positioning.** The positioning and strategies of UNDP are analysed both from the perspective of the organization's mandate and the development needs and priorities in the country as agreed and as they emerged. This will entail systematic analysis of the UNDP position within the development and policy space in the country, as well as strategies used by UNDP to maximize its contribution through adopting relevant strategies and approaches. The following criteria will be applied:

  - **Relevance and responsiveness** of the county programme as a whole to the challenges and needs of the country;

  - Use of the **comparative strengths** of UNDP;

  - Promoting the values of the **United Nations** from a human development perspective.

In addition to assessments made using the criteria above, the ADR process also identified how various factors can explain the performance of UNDP. The following general factors are considered in all ADRs:

- National context, political environment, conflict and security;

- National ownership of initiatives and results and use of national capacities;

- Gender equality and women's empowerment as preconditions for sustainable human development;

- South-South solutions and cooperation;

- Management and operations including programme management, human resource management and financial management.

Specific attention was paid to UNDP support to furthering gender equality and women's empowerment in Somalia in agreement with the United Nations System-wide Action Plan on Gender Equality and the Empowerment of Women (UN SWAP).[7] In addition, the evaluation also examined a number of other factors[8] that are assumed

---

7   http://www.unwomen.org/en/how-we-work/un-system-coordination/promoting-un-accountability.

8   Identified in consultation with the county office and Regional Bureau for Arab States.

to have had an impact on the performance of UNDP over the last four and one half years (2011-2015):

a) The implications of the relocation of staff, including senior management, to and from Mogadishu;

b) Security issues and associated limitations to implementation (including monitoring);

c) Selection of implementation modalities and monitoring in the context of remote management;

d) Gender perspectives of the country office business environment;

e) The role in the integrated mission, coordination issues and joint work;

f) Support from headquarters[9] and the regional service centre.

The unit of analysis for the evaluation is the country programme outcome, as specified in the CPD. Progress towards the respective outcomes between 2011 and March 2015 and the UNDP contribution to that change is examined.

The evaluation took into account the fact that although the projects are centrally managed, different elements are implemented in each of the areas covered by the country office in Mogadishu and the two area offices in Garowe and Hargeisa. Efforts were made to make separate assessments of each of these areas as well as of the overall programme.

1.3 DATA COLLECTION

Assessment of data collection constraints and existing data. Early in the ADR process, an assessment was carried out for each country programme outcome to ascertain the available information and identify data constraints so as to determine the data collection needs and methods. The assessment outlined the level of evaluable data that is available and indicated that: (a) six evaluations were commissioned by the country office since the start of the 2011-2015 country programme and completed in time for use by the ADR.[10] Although there are no outcome evaluations, Somalia has been a case study in two recent evaluations commissioned by the Bureau for Crisis Prevention and Recovery;[11] (b) systematic monitoring of outcomes is available for the evaluation to build on; and (c) monitoring of outputs has sometimes been challenging due to security reasons. The data collection methods and tools aim to address the data gaps, as well as the policy-level information not covered in existing evaluations.

The security situation in parts of the county presented practical challenges to data collection and heavily influenced the approach undertaken by the evaluation team. The UNDP Country Director and Deputy Country Director (Programme) returned to Mogadishu a month before the start of the main data collection mission in June 2014 and re-opened offices in the United Nations Common Compound. Some staff are located in the Mogadishu International Airport compound to be near the United Nations Assistance Mission in Somalia (UNSOM).[12]

Data collection methods. The key methods used are document review, key informant interviews and observations during field visits. The key informant interviews involved government representatives, civil society organizations (CSOs), private sector representatives, United Nations

---

9   Specifically, the Regional Bureau for Arab States, the Bureau for Development Policy and the Bureau for Crisis Prevention and Recovery. The latter two units were merged to form the Bureau for Policy and Programme Support in late 2014.

10   Including evaluations of the Somali Institutional Development Project and joint programme on local governance.

11   UNDP reintegration programmes and UNDP-supported mobile courts interventions (Somaliland).

12   These arrangements are described in more detail in chapter 3.

agencies, multilateral organizations, bilateral donors and beneficiaries of the programme. The list of persons met can be found in annex 2. The desk review covered background documents on the national context, documents prepared by international partners during the period under review and documents prepared by United Nations system agencies; programme plans and frameworks; progress reports; monitoring self-assessments such as the UNDP results-oriented annual report (ROAR); and evaluations conducted by the country office and partners. This list of documents consulted can be found in annex 4.

The core team of IEO staff and consultants visited Mogadishu, Garowe, Gardo and Hargeisa in June 2014. Due to the security situation, there was limited time or opportunity for engaging with the national authorities and other stakeholders in Mogadishu compared with the other areas visited. In addition, a consulting firm was contracted to undertake project-level data collection in areas outside those visited by the core team. In each of the three regions, two consultants visited between three and four project sites covering between 9 and 11 small projects or project components. The criteria for selecting places for field visits included: accessibility/security; critical mass of project interventions; potential for significant learning (both successful as well as challenging cases); and coverage of all programme areas. A list of projects and sites can be found in annex 3. The final report was delivered to IEO in mid-December 2014.[13]

The evaluation used a process of triangulation of information collected from different sources and/or by different methods to ensure that the data are valid. The evaluation team developed the findings, conclusions and recommendations based on the analysis of data.

1.4 MANAGEMENT ARRANGEMENTS AND PROCESS

The IEO conducted the ADR in consultation with the Somalia country office, the Regional Bureau for Arab States (RBAS) and the Federal Government of Somalia.[14] The IEO evaluation managers led the evaluation and coordinated the evaluation team which included two other IEO staff members, one with specific reasonability for examining management and operations issues. In addition, a gender specialist consultant formed part of the core team. Government counterparts of UNDP in Somalia facilitated the conduct of the ADR by providing necessary access to information sources within the Government.

The UNDP country office supported the evaluation team to liaise with key partners and other stakeholders, make available to the team all necessary information regarding UNDP programmes, projects and activities in the country, and provide factual verifications of the draft report on a timely basis. The country office (and the area offices) provided the evaluation team in-kind support (e.g., arranging meetings with project staff, stakeholders and beneficiaries; and assistance for the project site visits). To ensure the independence of the views expressed in interviews and meetings with stakeholders held for data collection purposes, country office staff did not participate. The RBAS supported the evaluation through information-sharing and participated in discussions on emerging conclusions and recommendations. The process is described in more detail in the terms of reference (annex 1).

The IEO team held feedback meetings with the senior management of UNDP Somalia in November 2014 and with RBAS in August 2014. The report on gender and the three project–level data collection reports were shared when they became ready and the draft of the complete ADR

---

13 Some delays resulted from the difficulty in getting subproject information in Garowe, Gardo and Mogadishu.

14 Where reference is made to the Federal Government of Somalia, the ADR also recognizes the Somaliland Special Arrangement as set out in the New Deal Compact.

CHAPTER 1. INTRODUCTION

report was shared in April 2015. Due to the six-month difference between the main data collection mission and the completion of field work, it was decided to have a final mission in June 2015 to ensure consistency across all the timelines and bring the report up to date. This was especially important due to the need to capture the various alignment processes as well as significant efforts that had been made by the country office management during this period. For security reasons, the IEO decided not to hold a physical stakeholder workshop in Somalia at the end of the evaluation process. The report is expected to be made available to the Executive Board in 2017.

1.5 LIMITATIONS AND CHALLENGES

The ADR found it challenging to apply fully United Nations Evaluation Group standards related to measurement of inputs, outputs and outcomes when presenting findings. UNDP monitoring and reporting of results tended to be better formulated at the activity and output results levels. This was partly due to the limited use of appropriate outcome indicators (e.g., change in institutional performance, change in sector coordination, behaviour change, etc.). That made it difficult to systematically measure the contribution of UNDP and to show the progression from implementation to outcome results. Also, previous evaluations were at the project level and therefore evidence on progress towards outcomes was not available. The ADR thus draws on stakeholders' perceptions which have been triangulated and cross-verified by the different sources to assess the effectiveness of UNDP.

1.6 STRUCTURE OF THE REPORT

The second chapter sets out the national development context over the period being examined and is followed by the third chapter on the UNDP programme being evaluated and how it evolved over time. Chapter four sets out the main findings related to the assessment of UNDP performance by each of the outcomes found in the 2011-2015 CPD. Chapter five examines two sets of factors affecting performance that are common across all outcomes, namely, management and operational issues and issues related to the strategic positioning of UNDP in Somalia. Chapter six sets out the conclusions (key messages emerging from an interpretation of the findings) and recommendations for future action.

Chapter 2

NATIONAL CONTEXT

This chapter introduces the country context within which UNDP has operated since 2010, from the period just before the start of the new country programme. Its purpose is to facilitate assessment of the performance of UNDP, for example on relevance. It is broad in scope with specific context related to the UNDP areas of interventions set out in chapter 4.

2.1 POLITICAL DEVELOPMENTS

The most significant political development in Somalia since the start of the country programme is the restructuring of governance around a federal system. Somalia witnessed a series of transitional governments between 2000 and 2012 which were mandated to federalize the country. In 2012, the country marked the end of the transition by adopting a Provisional Constitution and electing a new Parliament. The political framework stipulated in the Constitution and endorsed by the Somali Compact[15] for a consensus-based transition to democracy was called Vision 2016. The priorities of Vision 2016 are: (a) the formation of federal states through peaceful reconciliation; (b) the finalization and adoption of the Constitution; and (c) preparation for national elections in 2016.

The federalization process gained momentum in 2014 with three interim regional administrations formed between 2014 and 2015. Negotiations on the formation of a fourth interim regional administration (comprising Hiiraan and Middle Shabelle regions) are ongoing. Puntland, an autonomous region since 1998, constitutes the only full-fledged federal state. As interim regional administrations are expected to transition to become federal member states with parliamentary approval, the federalization process is far from complete as of mid-2015.

Since 2012, talks have been ongoing between the Federal Government of Somalia and Somaliland to reach a settlement on the status of the latter. Somaliland, which declared unilateral independence in 1991, has not been recognized internationally and has a 'special arrangement' under the existing political framework supported by the international community.

The two other State-building priorities of Vision 2016 are also unlikely to be completed by August 2016. The Provisional Constitution was expected to be reviewed, finalized and eventually put to a public referendum; however, it has proven to be technically complicated[16] and there has been little progress. Similarly, preparations, including voter registration, for the envisioned direct elections at the end of the term of the incumbent President, Hassan Sheikh Mohamoud, in August 2016 had not begun.[17]

---

15   The Somali Compact, based on the Federal Government's Six Pillar Policy, was signed between the Federal Government and the international community in September 2013 and articulates Somalia's Peacebuilding and State-building Goals for the period 2014-2016. The Compact is based on the Busan New Deal principles (http://www.newdeal4peace.org/about-the-new-deal/).

16   Schmidt, J, 'Vision 2016 in Autumn 2015: What can still be achieved in the Somali peace- and state-building process?', ConstitutionNet.org, October 2015.

17   In July 2015 the Federal Government of Somalia announced that direct elections will not be possible in 2016 and alternative models will need to be looked at. See VOA, 29 July 2015, http://www.voanews.com/content/somalia-says-no-popular-election-in-2016/2883749.html

The difficulties which the Federal Government of Somalia faced in implementing Vision 2016 are largely rooted in the challenges emanating from the institutional breakdown and fragmentation of Somali society following the collapse of the last functional Somali Government in 1991. Lack of consensus among the political elites on the issues at hand and continued infighting in the Government resulted in multiple cabinet reshuffles. Consequently, key independent commissions required to lead constitutional review and federalization could not be formed on time. The Constitution itself has generated more confusion than clarity on roles and responsibilities between different levels of government. There is also critique of the process of the Somali Compact and Vision 2016, with the planning and target-setting said to be externally driven[18] and rushed at the expense of consultation with a wider group of Somali stakeholders, a prerequisite for national reconciliation and peacebuilding.[19] Corruption is systemic and an underlying cause of many of the problems threatening the development of effective governance institutions in Somalia.[20]

civilians remain the major source of insecurity in these regions. The security situation in Puntland and Somaliland has been relatively more stable since the mid-1990s, although Puntland has been witnessing increased incidence of terrorist attacks since 2013.[21]

The partial lifting of the arms embargo by the Security Council on 6 March 2013 and the extension of the African Union Military Observer Mission in Somalia (AMISOM)[22] has enabled the Government to strengthen its security forces with light weapons in the fight against terrorism. Significant military gains made against Al-Shabaab between 2013 and 2015 by AMISOM and the Somali Army have made the group marginally weaker operationally, although it continues to wage attacks and restrict humanitarian access by blockading key towns and supply routes.[23] Al-Shabaab attacks have also spread to Kenya. Funding challenges facing both AMISOM and the Somali National Army in the face of an Al-Shabaab rebound is worrying.[24] The Security Council extended the mandate of AMISOM until May 2016.

2.2   PEACE AND SECURITY SITUATION

Insecurity remains a problem throughout the south and central regions, hindering humanitarian and development assistance. Al-Shabaab attacks against the Government, its partners and

2.3   ECONOMIC CONTEXT

As a result of two-decade conflict and the resulting collapse of the country's political and economic institutions, there is a drastic lack of basic economic and social statistics. No comprehen-

---

18   Mosley, J, 'Somalia's Federal Future: Layered Agendas, Risks and Opportunities', Chatham House, Royal Institute for International Affairs, September 2015.

19   Center on International Cooperation, 'A Deal for Somalia? The Somali Compact and its Implications for Peacebuilding', New York University, July 2014.

20   United Nations Monitoring Group on Somalia and Eritrea, 'Report of the Monitoring Group on Somalia and Eritrea', October 2015. Also Somalia was ranked 174th of 175 countries in 2014 in Transparency International's Corruption Index.

21   41 incidents in 2012; 64 in 2013; 72 in 2014; 111 in 2015. Data attributed to the United Nations Safety and Security Department.

22   AMISOM is a regional peacekeeping mission operated by the African Union with the approval of the United Nations in 2007. AMISOM is mandated to conduct peace support operations in Somalia to stabilize the situation in the country in order to create conditions for the conduct of humanitarian activities. An immediate takeover by the United Nations was foreseen but did not materialize.

23   Somalia Newsroom: "Is al-Shabaab Stronger or Weaker after Godane's Death?". September 2014. https://somalianewsroom.com/2014/09/22/analysis-is-al-shabaab-stronger-or-weaker-after-godanes-death/

24   United Nations Monitoring Group on Somalia and Eritrea, 'Report of the Monitoring Group on Somalia and Eritrea', October 2015.

sive household income and expenditure survey has been conducted for many years. Although difficult to quantify, the gross domestic product (GDP) of Somalia was estimated at about $5.4 billion in 2013, with an average per capita GDP of $435.[25] UNDP programme documents quote a much lower per capita income of $226.[26]

Somalia's economy is dominated by the informal sector and is predominantly based on agriculture and livestock, which account for about 65 per cent of GDP and employment of the workforce.[27] With an overwhelming pastoralist economy, livestock represents the family's wealth and has traditionally been the property of men, although women often manage the sale and exchange of livestock products such as milk and ghee and spend their earnings on household needs. There is also reliance on remittances from abroad, which are estimated to provide support to about 40 per cent of the population.

With the collapse of the central Government, the private sector maintained Somalia's economy. It demonstrated resilience and vitality in areas such as telecommunications, transportation, livestock and fisheries. In this context, the extensive Somali diaspora has played a major role by injecting a significant inflow of funds through a well-established, relatively cheap, efficient and trusted transfer system.[28] The majority of public services are offered by individual suppliers including a dynamic financial sector, water, electricity and other vital services in stable areas. Various private telecommunications companies which sprang up in the early 2000s in the absence of public-owned infrastructure have gained a foothold and taken advantage of technological innovations to branch into banking services. Leading telecommunications companies across Somalia now offer mobile money transfer services to customers, facilitating the speed and ease of business transactions. The number of mobile subscriptions in Somalia is estimated at about 51 per 100 people.[29]

2.4 THE STATUS OF HUMAN DEVELOPMENT

Somalia does not have a national development plan. In 2015 the Federal Government of Somalia launched a process to develop such a plan, compliant to the standard of an interim poverty reduction strategy paper, which would succeed the current Somali Compact. In doing so, the Government has shown strong interest in shifting towards longer-term development and alignment with the Sustainable Development Goals. The National Development Plan (NDP) will be the first comprehensive planning effort in more than two decades and represents an opportunity for more meaningful development responses, in parallel with humanitarian and peacebuilding interventions. Both Puntland and Somaliland are implementing five-year national development plans, respectively for 2014-2018 and 2012-2016.

Somalia's current population is estimated at 12.3 million people, with an annual growth rate of 2.9 per cent between 1990 and 2013. Forty-two per cent of the population is estimated to be urban, 49 per cent rural/nomadic and 9 per cent are internally displaced persons.[30] Over 1 million Somalis reside in the diaspora, especially in Canada, the United States, the United Kingdom, the

---

25 World Bank and International Monetary Fund estimates. See World Bank, 'Somalia Economic Update: Transition amid Risks', October 2015.

26 E.g., UNDP Somalia 2013 Annual Report.

27 African Development Bank Group, 'Somalia Country Brief 2013-2015', March 2013.

28 See UNDP, 'Cash and Compassion: The role of the Somali Diaspora in Relief, Development and Peacebuilding', December 2011.

29 World Bank, World Bank Development Indicators database, 2014.

30 United Nations Population Fund (UNFPA), Population Estimate Survey, 2014. Although the Federal Government endorsed and launched the survey results, it is important to note that they were contested by the public.

Netherlands, Scandinavian countries and neighbouring Kenya, Ethiopia and Djibouti.[31]

As a summary of its development status, the 2013 Millennium Development Goal report shows that Somalia was unlikely to achieve all but one of its targets, that being the reduction in child mortality (under-five mortality rate reduced by two thirds between 1990 and 2015). Using another summary of development status, the Human Development Index ranked Somalia 165 of 170 countries in the 2010 global Human Development Report.[32]

The Multidimensional Poverty Index (MPI) identifies multiple deprivations in the form of indicators of health, education and standard of living for each person surveyed. Findings by the United Nations indicate that about 82 per cent of nomadic Somalis are poor across multiple dimensions. Somalia's MPI is 0.47, placing Somalia at 94 of 104 countries in the 2010 global Human Development Report. Somalia's low MPI can be attributed mainly to low standards of living (50 per cent), followed by low levels of education and dismally low access to good health (19 per cent). Overall, 73 per cent of Somalis live on under $2 per day.[33]

Rates of acute child malnutrition (affecting one in six children) are among the highest in the world.[34] Somalia has been food insecure for the past 20 years, a situation which has been aggravated by civil war and natural disasters. Drought and resulting famine last struck the Horn of Africa in 2011, when 3.2 million people in Somalia alone required emergency humanitarian assistance. Said to be the worst in 60 years, the drought caused a severe food crisis across Somalia resulting in thousands of deaths. Many refugees from southern Somalia fled to neighbouring Kenya and Ethiopia, where crowded, unsanitary conditions led to additional fatalities. The last significant drought in the Horn of Africa before 2011 was in 2005.

2.5 GENDER EQUALITY AND WOMEN'S EMPOWERMENT

Despite the existence of overall conducive constitutional and policy frameworks at the federal level and in Puntland and Somaliland, Somalia's record on women's human rights is weak. In the aftermath of the civil war, Somali women have assumed greater roles in social and economic recovery but this has not been commensurate with their participation in public decision-making, which remains limited. The proportion of parliamentary seats held by women is very low (14 per cent in the federal national Parliament; 3 per cent in Puntland; 1.2 per cent in Somaliland; and 4 per cent in the Interim Jubba Administration).[35] There are no women in the Interim South West Administration's parliament. The main constraint remains a patrilineal clan-based society blending traditional nomadic and Islamic norms. A woman's identity and status shift through her life cycle; as an unmarried woman, she is a member of her father's household and as a married woman she moves to her husband's family. This ambiguity over women's identity creates uncertainty over their allegiance in decision-making dominated by clan systems.

Other challenges faced by Somali women include discriminatory attitudes rooted in cultural practices which see women as intellectual minors. Gender-based violence, including female genital mutilation/cutting (FGM/C) and sexual violence, is widespread. The human rights system and architecture are still weak and do not prioritize such violations. Instead, customary law, which

---

31 UNDP, 'Somalia's Missing Million: The Somalia Diaspora and its role in Development', Nairobi, 2009.

32 UNDP, 'Somalia Human Development Report 2012: Empowering youth for peace and development', Nairobi, 2012.

33 Ibid.

34 UNDP country programme document (2011-2015).

35 UNDP Somalia.

is often contradictory to international human rights principles, is used to settle cases such as rape, divorce and homicide. Women's access to health services is limited, and Somalia's maternal mortality ratio is one of the highest in the world, at 850 per 100,000 live births (2013 World Bank modelled estimate). According to the World Health Organization, approximately 98 per cent of women in Somalia undergo FGM/C, and it is performed mostly on girls between the ages of 4 and 11 years in its most severe form; infibulation is reported to be practiced in 80 per cent of cases.

2.6 THE ENVIRONMENT

With agriculture and livestock as the mainstays of the Somali economy, the country is heavily dependent on the environment and natural resources for economic growth. Somalia still has relatively weak institutional frameworks for environmental protection and natural resources management. For these reasons, environmental degradation, natural disasters and climate change remain the greatest threat to livelihoods, food security, peace and stability. The recurrent and devastating droughts and the irregular and varying seasonal rainfalls continue to jeopardize efforts aimed at food security and poverty alleviation, with far reaching implications for the broader humanitarian situation and peace and stability in the region.

The link between conflict and natural resources in Somalia is well established and had largely remained an internal matter. Control and access to scarce natural resources, e.g., land and water, have been traditional sources of conflict in all the Somali territories. In the south and central regions, Al-Shabaab's recent control of territory including some of the best agricultural land had subdued intercommunal conflict over natural resources, but with the group pushed out of these territories and power vacuums emerging, resource-based conflicts are resurfacing.

Meanwhile, the conflict could be taking on international and regional dimensions. With reported potential for oil and gas,[36] there is growing international interest in Somalia's mineral resources which could lead to exploitation as well as new conflicts in the country and in the region.[37] The exploitation of Somalia's maritime resources had in the past triggered piracy. The country has the longest coastline in Africa and no control over its 200-nautical-mile exclusive economic zone, which has significant productive fishing capacity. Illegal fishing had decreased due to piracy but is on the rise again following international security interventions against piracy. Returning shipping fleets are now armed and, taking advantage of the limited ability of the Somali Government to monitor its shores, continue with illegal fishing activities.[38] This also poses a risk of continued conflict on Somalia's seas.[39]

The Somali charcoal trade fuels both environmental degradation and conflict in the country. The international trade is particularly lucrative and many powerful people profit from it over and beyond Al-Shabaab, including, according to some, some members of the Kenyan military[40] present in the concerned areas (mainly around Kismayo).[41] The charcoal in question is of particularly high quality and in high demand in Gulf markets for the flavour it gives to meat.

---

36 African Development Bank Group, 'Somalia Country Brief 2013-2015', (2013), citing "some surveys".

37 Ibid.

38 United Nations, 'Report of the Monitoring Group on Somalia and Eritrea', October 2015.

39 Ibid.

40 Report of the Monitoring Group on Somalia and Eritrea pursuant to Security Council resolution 2060 (S/2013/413), p.9. http://www.un.org/ga/search/view_doc.asp?symbol=S/2013/413 .

41 Somalia Water and Land Information Management (SWALIM) Update Quarterly Newsletter, May - July 2013, Issue 2: SWALIM Locates Source of the Kismayo Charcoal Pile, at http://reliefweb.int/sites/reliefweb.int/files/resources/SWALIM%20Update%20Issue%202.pdf .

2.7 INTERNATIONAL DEVELOPMENT SUPPORT FOR SOMALIA

The major international support comes from the United Nations and the African Union. In 2010, United Nations political support came through the United Nations Political Office for Somalia (UNPOS) which had been established to help advance peace and reconciliation in the country. In May 2013, the Security Council[42] established UNSOM to provide the United Nations 'good offices' functions and a range of strategic policy advice in support of the Federal Government's peace and reconciliation process. The mandate of UNSOM includes the provision of policy advice to the Federal Government and AMISOM on peace-building and State-building.[43] UNSOM is the first United Nations political mission based in Somalia since 1994 and on 1 January 2014 the United Nations in Somalia was structurally integrated.

Somalia is also a member of the Intergovernmental Authority on Development (IGAD), which was established in 1986 to encourage cooperation among Member States in East Africa. Specifically, IGAD encourages increased cooperation through: (a) food security and environmental protection; (b) promotion and maintenance of peace and security and humanitarian affairs; and (c) economic cooperation and integration.

Official development assistance (ODA). In addition to the military and political support of the international community, Somalia has received significant ODA resources from the international community as illustrated in figure 1.

The Somali Compact. The Compact enshrines the principles for a renewed partnership between

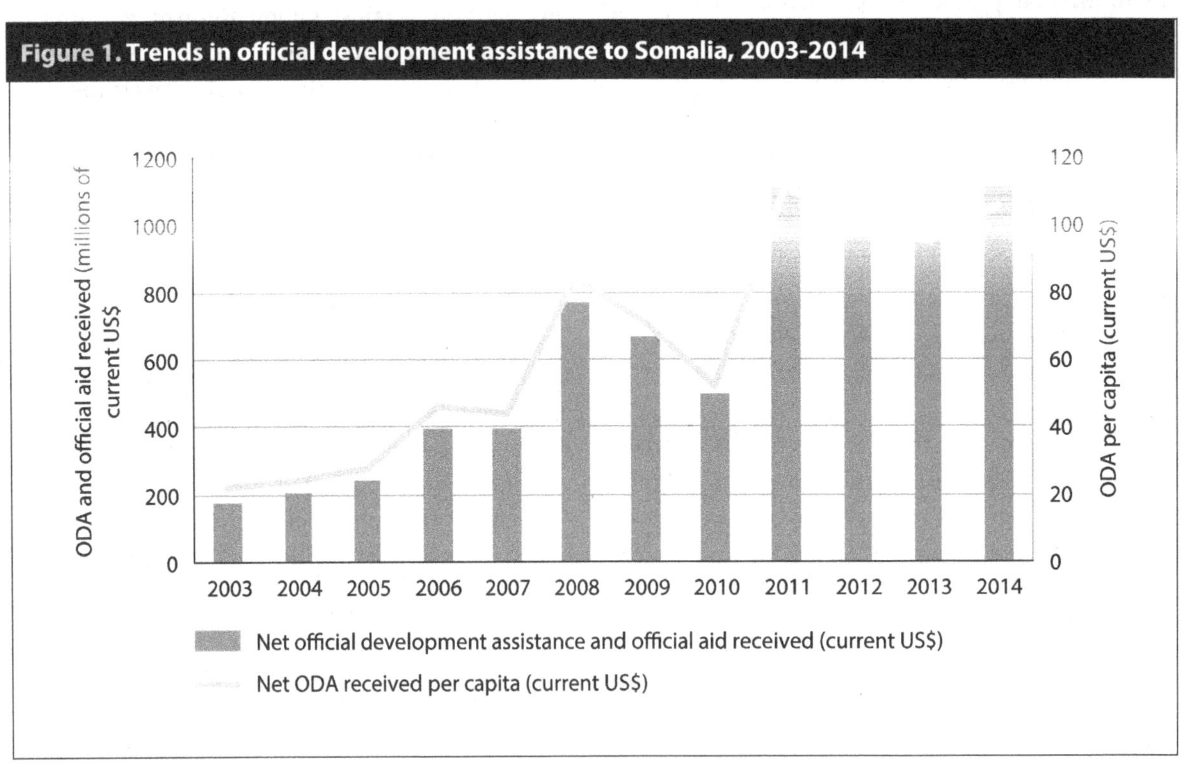

Figure 1. Trends in official development assistance to Somalia, 2003-2014

Source: World Bank

---

42   Security Council resolution 2102 (2013).

43   Specifically, in the areas of: (a) governance; (b) security sector reform and rule of law (including the disengagement of combatants); (c) development of a federal system (including preparations for elections in 2016); and (d) coordination of international donor support.

Somalia and the international community based on the New Deal for Engagement in Fragile States. The Compact articulates five Peacebuilding and State-building Goals (PSGs) for Somalia. These PSGs are elaborated and their implementation coordinated through working groups led by the Federal Government of Somalia, which include representatives of the Somali regions, interim regional administrations, federal states and international partners including the United Nations, Parliament and civil society. The PSGs cover:

a) inclusive politics (PSG1);

b) security (PSG2);

c) justice (PSG3);

d) economic foundations (PSG4);

e) revenues and services (PSG5).

The Compact includes a range of cross-cutting issues: gender; capacity development; bringing tangible results to the people (stabilization); respect for human rights; and external relations. It also includes a 'special arrangement' for Somaliland that takes into consideration its specific priorities and needs.

As part of the Compact, the Federal Government of Somalia and development partners agreed to establish the Somalia Development and Reconstruction Facility (SDRF) as a centrepiece of the New Deal partnership and in order to enhance the delivery of effective assistance to all Somalis. Closely aligned with the Somalia Compact principles, the SDRF serves as a mechanism for the Federal Government to oversee and guide the diverse activities of its development partners. The SDRF will bring together several funds ('windows') under common governance arrangements and will be administered by the United Nations, the World Bank and the African Development Bank.

ODA fraud and corruption. Concerns have been reported about the handling of international development assistance support for Somalia. According to the 2013 audit of the management by the

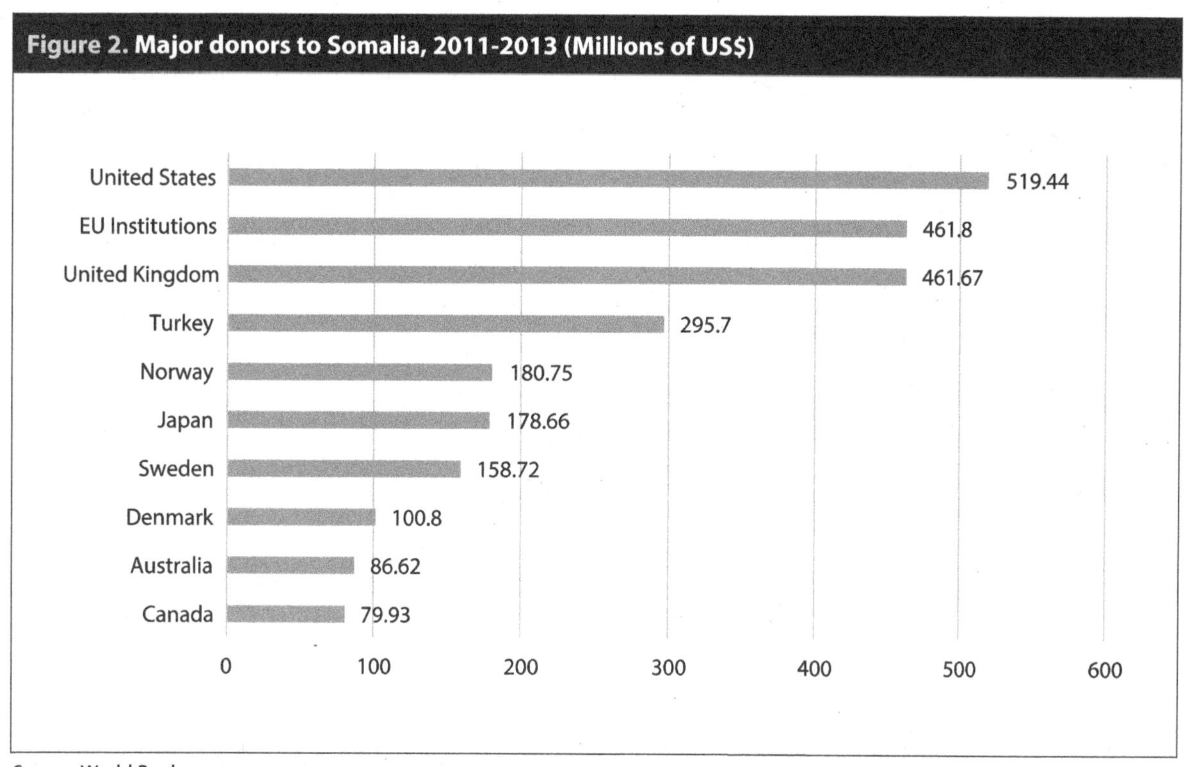

Figure 2. Major donors to Somalia, 2011-2013 (Millions of US$)

Source: World Bank

United Nations Office for the Coordination of Humanitarian Assistance (OCHA) of the Common Humanitarian Fund for Somalia, undertaken by the United Nations Office of Internal Oversight Services, OCHA could not provide assurance that the money it spent in Somalia as part of the Common Humanitarian Fund was used for the intended purposes.[44] In its resolution 1972 (2011), the Security Council called on Member States and the United Nations to take all possible steps to mitigate the politicization, the misuse and the misappropriation of humanitarian assistance in Somalia and requested reporting on the implementation of such measures. The United Nations Country Team (UNCT) in Somalia adopted an enterprise risk management framework and since 2011 has had an established Risk Management Unit. The Unit is tasked with ensuring effective, efficient and harmonized assistance to the people of Somalia while mitigating risks associated with the delivery of assistance entrusted to the United Nations system.

---

44 Office of Internal Oversight Services, Audit of the Office for the Coordination of Humanitarian Affairs (OCHA) Managing Agent Role for the Somalia Common Humanitarian Fund, report 2014/078, August 2014.

Chapter 3

THE UNDP RESPONSE THROUGH ITS COUNTRY PROGRAMME

The purpose of the chapter is to describe the UNDP programmatic response to the context through the ongoing country programme (2011-2015) and the implementation of the programme itself. The chapter includes analysis of the management arrangements and the changes that have taken place in the past five years. In so doing, it will support the assessment of how such programming and management arrangements have affected performance discussed in chapter 5. It also indicates how UNDP used the findings, conclusions and recommendations of the previous ADR in designing the ongoing country programme.

3.1 THE UNDP COUNTRY PROGRAMME, 2011-2015

UNDP and the broader United Nations context in Somalia. Somalia joined the United Nations in September 1960 and was a member of the Security Council in 1971-1972. As noted in the previous chapter, the United Nations has played and continues to play a major role in the economic and political life of Somalia through its political missions, which are mandated by the Security Council to provide policy advice to the Government. There is also a strong United Nations development presence and a UNCT comprising 22 agencies, funds and programmes.

UNDP has been active in Somalia since 1977.[45] The previous country programme (2008-2009)

was extended to 2010 so it would be harmonized with the United Nations Transition Plan for Somalia. The new country programme (2011-2015) was developed in the framework of the United Nations Somalia Assistance Strategy (UNSAS) 2011-2015 and the Integrated Strategic Framework (ISF) 2014-2016. The UNSAS was developed as the foundation and framework for the work of United Nations agencies, funds and programmes from 2011 to 2015.

An important premise of the UNSAS was the need for a longer-term commitment to Somalia as opposed to what was perceived as excessive focus on the short term in the past. In nearly 20 years of conflict, insufficient attention has been given to its underlying causes. The UNSAS was therefore designed to give more space to the longer-term needs and aspirations of the Somali people, which should result in progress towards peace and development. Fully aligned with the UNSAS, the UNDP country programme also adopted such a longer-term approach.

In early 2014, the United Nations developed the ISF[46] for Somalia following the signature of the Somali Compact. The ISF, which replaces the UNSAS 2011-2015, sets out how the United Nations will contribute to the implementation of the Somali Compact. The process of developing the ISF was useful to all parts of the United Nations system, helping them to identify key areas where increased strategic integration was possible

---

45 'Agreement between the Government of the Somali Democratic Republic and the United Nations Development Programme', 31 May 1977.

46 The Integrated Assessment and Policy stipulates that the following planning documents are mandatory for United Nations integrated presences: (a) Directive to the Special or Executive Representative of the Secretary-General, Resident Coordinator and Humanitarian Coordinator, to be issued by Headquarters; and (b) an Integrated Strategic Framework. Both derive from an integrated assessment process. Ref IAP Working Group Integrated Assessment and Planning Handbook, December 2013.

and desirable. The United Nations system developed structures to guide implementation of the ISF and promote strategic integration.[47]

UNDP Somalia also needs to comply with the UN SWAP, which constitutes the first accountability framework for gender mainstreaming in the United Nations system. It is designed to define, monitor and drive progress towards a common set of standards for the achievement of gender equality and the empowerment of women.

The UNDP country programme, 2011-2015. The UNDP country programme was approved by the UNDP Executive Board at the second regular session of 2010. Aligned with the time frame of the UNSAS, the programme was planned for five years, recognizing that in order to achieve its development goals in Somalia, UNDP must be committed to investing time and resources for results that may not be realized in the short term. The programme was expected to contribute to four broad outcomes as illustrated in table 1.

Strategically, the design of the new country programme took into account two key recommendations of the previous ADR. The first recommendation was that "UNDP Somalia needs to re-anchor its country programme to areas which build on its core competence and are central to its mandate. It should work towards finding an alternative 'provider' or mechanism to take over activities related to providing services to political processes or for simple administrative functions which are not central to its mandate." The new country programme took UNDP in the recommended direction. The second recommendation was that "The next county programme for Somalia should strike an appropriate balance between intervention in support of building capacity of government institutions and initiatives to help address, in the short and medium term, the chronic development needs of the vulnerable groups of population, with a view to achieving progress towards the [Millennium Development Goals], including on pressing issues related to environment". The new country programme responded with an increase in expectations for funding livelihood programmes in Somalia.

Since the country programme was to be implemented in the three areas supported by the three sub-offices/area offices,[48] it was decided that a traditional country programme action plan (CPAP) signed by national authorities might not be appropriate. Specifically, the transition arrangements

Table 1. Country programme outcomes and indicative resources, 2011-2015		
Country programme outcome		**Indicative resources (Millions of US$)**
Outcome 1	Somali women and men and authorities are better able to build peace and manage conflict.	13.5
Outcome 2	Somali women and men, girls and boys benefit from more inclusive, equitable and accountable governance, improved services, human security, access to justice and human rights	110.75
Outcome 3	Somali women and men benefit from increased sustainable livelihood opportunities and improved natural resources management	83.3
Outcome 4	Somali women and men attain greater gender equality and are empowered.	12.45
	Total	**220**

Source: UNDP Somalia country programme document, 2011-2015 (DP/DCP/SOM/2)

---

47 Resident Coordinator Annual Report 2011.

48 The country office was still based in Nairobi at the time.

for the Transitional Government of Somalia were due to expire in August 2011 and it was difficult to foresee what would take its place. Instead the country office developed a 'CPD implementation plan' to serve as a planning tool.[49] The implementation plan comprised a narrative for each outcome and sub-outcome strategies, accompanied by tables detailing outputs and corresponding indicators under each outcome.

The development of sub-programmes. In Somalia, UNDP faces the challenge of operating with a medium-term vision in a context that requires considerable flexibility due to security, humanitarian and political factors. Political developments in Somalia that had taken place since the country programme was designed, as well as lessons learned from major areas of work, led to the development of a series of sub-programmes to help achieve the medium-term goals: (a) governance and rule of law; (b) poverty reduction and environmental protection; and (c) gender (which is both a programme and a cross-cutting issue). HIV and AIDS and peace and security are also considered cross-cutting issues. The relationship between these programmes and the four country programme outcomes is illustrated in table 2, which also sets out the components of the programmes. More details on the development, evolution and logic of each of these programmes, as well as the cross-cutting areas, can be found in the relevant sections of chapter 4.

Addressing gender equality in programming. A number of evaluation reports covering the previous programme, including the previous ADR, recommended the development of a dedicated capability to reinforce gender equality in all programmes. As a result, the country office developed a UNDP Somalia gender equality strategy, aligned with the 2011-2015 country programme, that contributed towards the gender equality outcomes defined by the UNDP Strategic Plan, 2008-2011, the global corporate strategy on gender equality, 2008–2013, the UNDP eight-point agenda for women's empowerment and eight-point agenda for girls and women in crisis, and Security Council resolutions 1325, 1820, 1888 and 1889. This strategy was designed to guide gender mainstreaming in the implementation of the country programme. It describes how the country office will establish a system to integrate gender equality and women's empowerment in its policies, operations and programming for the

Table 2. Outcomes, programmes and cross-cutting issues						
Outcomes	**Programmes**	**Programme components**	**Cross-cutting**			
1	Governance and rule of law	• Local governance • Institutional development • Constitutional reform and parliament	Gender equality and women's empowerment		HIV and AIDS	Peace and security
2		• Civilian police • Access to justice • Community security				
3	Poverty reduction and environmental protection	• Private sector development • Local economic development • Human development/Millennium Development Goals • Environmental management				
4	Gender equality and women's empowerment					

Source: Interviews with country office staff/annual report

---

49 The request for this alternative planning approach was made in a letter from the Director of RBAS to the Associate Administrator (dated 31 January 2011), which noted that UNICEF and UNFPA also would not be signing a CPAP with national authorities.

next five years. In addition the country office developed a set of practical tools, activities and structures to help implement the strategy:

a) development of the 'gender mainstreaming made easy – handbook for programme staff';[50]

b) providing quick gender analysis in the design and implementation of all programmes and projects for UNDP Somalia;

c) training on gender mainstreaming for programme and operations staff as well as partners;

d) including a gender specialist/the gender unit in all important committees, i.e., Local Project Appraisal Committee and the country office realignment advisory group;

e) establishment of a gender focal team, plus the inclusion of a gender-specific section in quarterly project reports;

f) development of gender action plans for each of the three offices (Nairobi, Hargeisa and Garowe).

The country office also undertook assessments and ratings through the use of the gender marker and the Gender Equality Seal,[51] for which the country office received a 'High Silver' award in 2015.

The new ISF and linking to the Somali Compact. In late October 2014, the ISF 2014-2016 was signed by the Federal Government of Somalia, UNSOM and the UNCT. The ISF aims to guide the strategic management of the United Nations political, development, human rights and security activities in Somalia, taking appropriate account of humanitarian needs and activities. Specifically, it sets out the role of the United Nations in implementing the Somali Compact. In accordance with the Organization's commitment to the New Deal principle of 'One Vision, One Plan,' the ISF mirrors the Compact and sets out the United Nations contribution to each of the five PSGs and cross-cutting issues.

It is also intended to be the basis for ongoing discussions at the leadership level on United Nations system-wide challenges and strategies. The ISF is based on a shared conflict analysis and common understanding of the operational environment in Somalia. The ISF should lead to:[52]

a) maximizing the impact of limited resources based on a clear and mutually reinforcing division of labour between UNSOM and the various agencies and their focal points, based on their respective mandates;

b) a stronger adherence to, and shared understanding of, the normative framework(s) under which all parts of the United Nations system operate, making operations politically more astute, consistent and effective;

c) the development of common, clear policies around critical, sensitive, political issues with real programmatic implications for all relevant parts of the United Nations system;

d) a more informed, more complex and richer understanding of the Somali context across the United Nations system, even where activities and programmatic responses are distinct or separate;

e) a more coherent and focused engagement of the United Nations with Somali authorities and international partners on shared strategic objectives.

---

50 The handbook was developed in response to demand by programme staff as follow-up to a successful training where a number of gender mainstreaming tools were outlined, accompanied by exercises requiring staff members to apply them to case studies and scenarios drawn from projects in the country office. The handbook provides the tools alongside examples of the eventual products that should be achieved if they are applied properly. The handbook provides staff the opportunity to apply the tools to their real-life work as opposed to adapted scenarios.

51 The gender marker is a corporate UNDP tool for tracking financial allocation to gender equality and women's empowerment. The Gender Equality Seal is a corporate certification process that recognizes the good performance of country offices and units in delivering transformational gender equality results. The Seal offers three levels of certification: Gold, Silver and Bronze.

52 United Nations Somalia Integrated Strategic Framework 2014-2016.

The ISF is also the basis for the programmatic development of United Nations interventions in Somalia, and represents the Organization's programme pipeline for the Multi-Partner Trust Fund for Somalia (MPTF). The MPTF will be developed within the framework of the SDRF (described in the previous chapter). The MPTF organizes its programmatic and operational work according to the priorities identified under each PSG of the Somali Compact. It will cover activities throughout the five PSGs, recognizing the activities and mandates of the United Nations system throughout and will focus on immediate delivery, building resilience and capacity development as a comparative advantage in relation to the other windows.

In addition to channelling funds for programmatic activities, the MPTF will perform a coherence and alignment function for ongoing United Nations programmes. While existing programmes (both joint programmes and the programmes/projects of individual entities) will maintain their accountability, governance structure and current legal relationship as stand-alone programmes, they will be progressively subject to the common reporting standards required by the SDRF and be progressively placed under SDRF oversight. The United Nations system will strive to align the governance of its existing programmes to the SDRF governance, to the extent possible.

Following the approval of the New Deal Compact, UNDP began to organize its projects into the PSG structure. Where in some cases they cut across a PSG (for instance, the community security project), the country office gave further consideration as how best to align them. Each UNDP project began to develop strategies to align with the New Deal. UNDP hopes that the changes undertaken to align to the New Deal will improve its strategic role as a development partner (see table 3).

Alignment to the UNDP Strategic Plan. Finally, the county programme has had to align with the UNDP Strategic Plan, 2014-2017. This alignment is defined as "the implementation of real changes to focus, results, intervention strategies and management practices, to apply the engagement principles of the Strategic Plan and deliver progressively on the Plan's vision and outcomes".[53]

Table 3. Relationship between programmes, country programme outcomes and Somali Compact PSGs					
Programme	**PSG 1**	**PSG 2**	**PSG 3**	**PSG 4**	**PSG 5**
Governance and rule of law	• Parliament • Community security	• Civilian police	• Access to justice		• Local governance
Poverty reduction and environment				• Local economic development • Private sector development • Environmental management • Statistics & Economic Analysis	
Cross-cutting	• Gender • HIV/AIDS • Institutional development				

Source: UNDP Senior Management Retreat Report (4-5 September 2014)[54]

---

53   Alignment Handbook: A Guide to Key Concepts and their Application, Final Draft, 28 May 2014.

54   The above table represents the actual alignment and is slightly different from the alignment set out in the UNDP Somalia Annual Report 2013.

3.2 PROGRAMME MANAGEMENT ARRANGEMENTS

At the start of the ongoing country programme period, the UNDP country office was based in Nairobi for security reasons. The previous ADR recommended that "UNDP Somalia should increase the presence of Nairobi-based staff in the field by making full use of existing possibilities, including slots, and increase interaction with Somali counterparts by using temporary proximity hubs easily accessible for the authorities with the aim of ensuring timely decision-making and resolution of problems".

In 2012, UNDP began the process of formally moving its country office from Nairobi to Mogadishu and by the end of December 2012, the UNDP Country Director had relocated there, the first to do so since 1993. By the end of the first quarter of 2013, 12 senior posts had been moved to Mogadishu and at that time it was expected that by mid-2013, the bulk of the team would be in Mogadishu (with up to 25 international staff based there).[55] It was expected that despite the restricted ability to move around Mogadishu, the increased presence of its staff would strengthen the ability of UNDP to implement and monitor its projects.

The move of the country office to Mogadishu was repeatedly commended by various stakeholders and significantly strengthened the position of UNDP.[56] On 19 June 2013, terrorists attacked the United Nations Common Compound in Mogadishu and UNDP personnel were among the casualties. This resulted in the move of key staff members, including senior management, back to Nairobi.[57] The UNDP presence in Somaliland and Puntland has been more stable and consistent,[58] with 55 staff in Hargeisa and 40 in Garowe in 2014, when the ADR began. The security conditions permitted greater movement, which had the corresponding effect of allowing the UNDP staff greater ability to monitor and oversee projects.[59] However, in April 2015 the United Nations was once again the target of a terrorist attack in Garowe, leaving four staff dead. Following this attack the security threat levels were raised across Somalia.

The move of the UNDP Country Director back to the United Nations Common Compound in Mogadishu in mid-2014 meant that UNDP Somalia staff worked from five distinctive offices:

- Mogadishu, at the United Nations Common Compound, where the country office is located;

- Mogadishu, at the Mogadishu International Airport compound, where staff work with the UNSOM integrated mission;

- Garowe area office, which supports UNDP work in Puntland;

- Hargeisa area office, which supports UNDP work in Somaliland;

  Nairobi, where operations staff and some programme support staff are located.

One country programme in three distinct environments. It is important to note UNDP is de facto implementing programmes and projects in three distinct programming environments (federal level, Puntland and Somaliland) through a single country programme. The challenges, priorities and capacities in the three environments are different: both Somaliland and Puntland have functional institutional capacities and are implementing medium- to long-term development plans, while the Federal Government is rebuilding governance institutions.

---

55 Norwegian Agency for International Development (NORAD), 'Review of the Norwegian Support to Somalia though UNDP' NORAD Report 10/2013, Oslo, Norway, 2013.

56 Notwithstanding this, the Government of Somaliland would have preferred that UNDP top management for Somalia continue being based in Nairobi rather than in Mogadishu (NORAD).

57 The implications of this move are further discussed in chapter 5.

58 With the exception of the 2008 bombing of the Hargeisa office that led to a withdrawal of approximately one year.

59 Norad, 'Review of the Norwegian Support to Somalia though UNDP' Norad Report 10/2013, Oslo, Norway, 2013.

Working as part of an integrated United Nations mission. The United Nations became a structurally integrated team on 1 January 2014. New coordination structures were established within UNSOM, including an 'enabling platform' for strategic integration. UNSOM also contains a number of teams that are integrated with UNDP, including in the areas of rule of law, constitutional review and elections. UNSOM is headed by a Special Representative of the Secretary-General for Somalia with two deputies, one of whom is the UNDP Resident Representative who also serves as the Resident and Humanitarian Coordinator.

3.3 PROGRAMME IMPLEMENTATION

UNDP is implementing its programme in an environment that is both high-risk and fluid. For example, on 20 July 2011 – just over six months into the new country programme – the United Nations officially declared famine in two regions in the southern part of Somalia and by August, 4 million people were in crisis and 750,000 people were at a risk of starvation and living in famine conditions. Insecurity presents a significant operational risk for UNDP and its implementing partners in Somalia. Although Al-Shabaab has increasingly lost control of territory, there has been an increase in attacks targeting the Government and the international community, especially in urban areas.[60] Implementation also faces some fiduciary risks; findings related to these issues are discussed further in chapter 5.

Implementation mechanisms. As a result of the special situation in Somalia, specifically the security challenges and the lack of usual programming tools such as the CPAP, UNDP has had to develop specific implementation mechanisms. Although the country office operated under the overall umbrella of the direct implementation modality, 17 per cent of delivery in 2013 was implemented through government and non-

governmental organizations (NGOs) via letters of agreement and microcapital grant agreements ($6.6 million and $2.4 million, respectively).[61]

The letter of agreement modality, an alternative for engaging with the Government and its institutions, functions as a way for UNDP to contract with government entities in pursuit of joint goals. *"This lends itself to the Somali context because it permits UNDP to engage simultaneously with the Federal Government of Somalia, the Puntland government and the Somaliland government, despite the political ambiguities."*[62] UNDP believes that the letters of agreement allow it to accomplish more than it could by itself, with its limited presence on the ground, and at a lower cost. It was also assumed that letters of agreement would assist national institutions in building their capacities in such areas as finance, administration, procurement and human resources, thus contributing to development of effective, transparent and accountable national institutions. On the down-

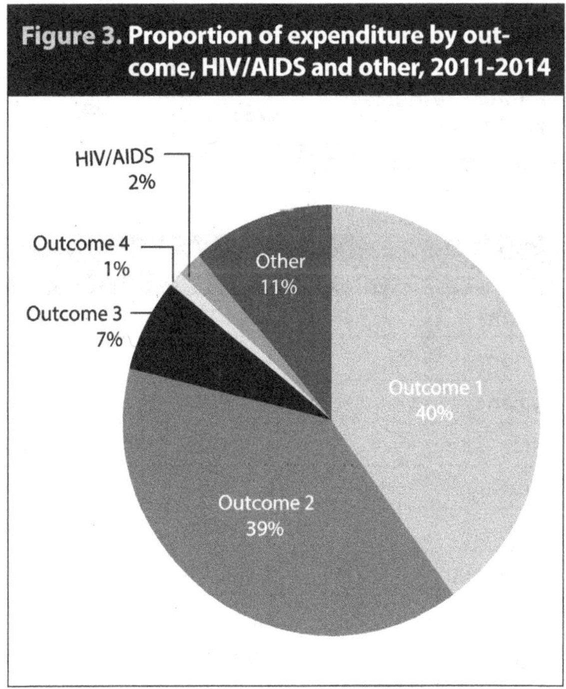

Figure 3. Proportion of expenditure by outcome, HIV/AIDS and other, 2011-2014

Source: UNDP Somalia Annual Reports 2011, 2012, 2013, and 2014

---

60 The security level in all areas was downgraded to Phase 3 after an April 2014 terrorist attack in Garowe, Puntland claimed the lives of four UNICEF staff.

61 2014 audit report.

62 NORAD, 'Review of the Norwegian Support to Somalia though UNDP' Norad Report 10/2013, Oslo, Norway, 2013.

side, they place a significant reporting and implementation burden on actors with very limited capacity. They are also difficult to monitor.

Financial resources. Total expenditures for the country programme for the four years from 2011 to 2014 were slightly higher than the indicative resources for the entire five-year period of the country programme for 2011-2015. Figure 3 illustrates expenditures for 2011-2014; it is clear that the vast majority of expenditures – about 80 per cent of the total – were through the governance and rule of law programme (representing outcomes 1 and 2). This contrasts with the expected allocation of 40 per cent of resources for the poverty reduction and environment programme at the time of the country programme design.

Only 11 per cent of UNDP programme resources are from regular resources and the rest were mobilized from a variety of donor and other international development organizations. As table 4 illustrates, this average nonetheless reflects a significant increase in the ration of regular to other resources from 7 per cent in 2011 to 18 per cent in 2014.

There is a high concentration on a small number of donors, with 57 per cent of all other resources contributions coming from just three donors (European Union, Japan and the United Kingdom) and nearly 75 per cent from the top six (Norway, Sweden and Denmark in addition to the three previously mentioned). Table 5 illustrates this pattern.

Table 4. Source of resources, 2011-2014 (expenditure, thousands of US$)

Source	2011	2012	2013	2014	Total	% of total
Regular resources	3,876	6,171	6,334	9,425	25,806	11%
Other resources	50,343	63,218	44,828	41,757	200,146	89%
Total	**54,219**	**69,389**	**51,162**	**51,182**	**225,952**	**100%**
Regular resources as % total	7%	9%	12%	18%	11%	

Source: Executive Snapshot

Table 5. Donor contributions, 2011-2014 (i.e., resources transferred to UNDP by year, in US$)

Donor	2011	2012	2013	2014	Total
European Union	15,944,550	9,717,019	14,534,260	5,203,635	45,399,464
Japan	12,406,224	11,610,606	8,300,000	8,902,933	41,219,763
United Kingdom*	4,881,882	7,167,058	12,130,841	9,055,240	33,235,021
Norway	7,079,495	-	5,750,904	3,858,834	16,689,233
Sweden	1,045,033	4,274,818	1,825,783	2,600,834	9,746,468
Denmark	1,344,809	2,547,449	2,716,162	3,669,260	10,277,680
United States	1,800,000	1,500,000	—	—	3,300,000
Italy	726,744	621,891	—	140,438	1,489,073
Australia	501,002	486,855	—	—	987,857
Ireland	—	389,610	—	—	389,610
All others	18,905,339	9,401,586	9,785,191	8,131,873	46,223,989
Grand total	**64,635,078**	**47,716,892**	**55,043,141**	**41,563,047**	**208,958,158**

* Department for International Development (DFID) + Foreign and Commonwealth Office.
Source: UNDP Somalia country office, Partnership and Planning Unit

Monitoring, evaluation and reporting. The previous ADR recommended that UNDP Somalia should pursue a conscious strategy to enhance the quality of programme planning and the delivery of results and financial resources. Specifically, it recommended that UNDP should: (a) mainstream a results-oriented culture through monitoring and evaluation (M&E) by ensuring that all programme staff are trained in M&E; (b) seek the necessary M&E technical expertise; and (c) assure adequate institutional arrangements and incentives.

The subsequent CPD stated that in accordance with the ADR, "UNDP Somalia commits to continue to improve its accountabilities through enhanced monitoring and evaluation, thereby ensuring a more effective oversight, especially where accessibility remains a challenge. As part of this effort, a Monitoring and Evaluation Unit will be established and an Oversight and Compliance Adviser will be recruited. This will be accompanied by a more astute focus on improved results-based management and result reporting. Insecurity is likely to remain a significant obstacle limiting the exposure and contact of UNDP 'in-country' with key government agencies, implementing partners, community representatives and with the Somali people in general. As a result, some quality assurance functions have been devolved upon a local oversight agency for monitoring and evaluation purposes".

Initially a system of third-party monitoring was established for poverty reduction and environment projects but was stopped around the same time that UNDP moved back to Mogadishu.

As a result, monitoring relied on project systems where they existed. In 2011 the country office also started to prepare annual reports that present an overall narrative report on the achievements of UNDP during the past year.

In 2013 the country office recruited a P-3 M&E Specialist. A two-year M&E workplan (2015-2016) that includes third-party monitoring and verification, output-level surveys and annual perception surveys was prepared in 2014. The office is recruiting two national M&E analysts to strengthen this area (ROAR 2014). In addition, in 2014 UNDP developed and launched a Community Security Index to measure the effectiveness and social impact of the governance and rule of law interventions (community security, justice and policing) in the target districts in order to understand the overall impact of the area-based interventions. At the time of the evaluation, the index was not fully operational but it will utilize the strengths of local governance structures in order to develop a sustainable mechanism to collect information at the district level to determine the social impact of governance and rule of law interventions. The pilot phase has been completed and mixed reviews were received from UNDP staff. The country office intends to improve the quality of data produced in the coming waves of data collection. In 2015, UNDP reported launching a third-party monitoring approach for its projects across Somalia. A national partner was engaged to undertake field verification and call centre verification across all projects. The country office also redesigned its reporting template to ensure inclusion of all monitoring and oversight activities and evidence throughout its reporting.

THE UNDP CONTRIBUTION TO DEVELOPMENT RESULTS

This chapter examines and assesses the UNDP contribution to development results as well as the quality of that contribution using the evaluation criteria set out in chapter 1: effectiveness; efficiency; sustainability; and relevance. First, the effectiveness of UNDP is presented by each of the four country programme outcome results and for HIV and AIDS, which is a cross-cutting issue. The quality of the contribution is then assessed by relevance, efficiency and sustainability across the entire programme.

4.1 EFFECTIVENESS OF THE UNDP CONTRIBUTION

4.1.1 POVERTY REDUCTION AND ENVIRONMENTAL PROTECTION

> **Planned outcome result:** Somali women and men benefit from increased sustainable livelihood opportunities and improved natural resources management.

Overview

As noted above, Somalia's economy is largely dependent on the informal sector. Agriculture and livestock account for about 65 per cent of GDP and employment of the workforce in all Somali sub-entities. The main products include sorghum and corn, live animals, fish, charcoal, bananas and sugar.[63] The country is thus heavily dependent on natural resources for livelihoods and economic growth. Some of the country's most fertile lands, the Shebelle and Juba valleys, have been the sites of some of the most damaging armed conflicts. A diminishing natural resource base and the unregulated exploitation of scarce resources contribute to further conflict over access.[64]

According to a recent environmental assessment by the United States Agency for International Development (USAID),[65] the most pressing environmental issues in Somalia today are land degradation, inadequate access to safe water and urban waste. Land degradation is caused by overgrazing, wood harvesting and charcoaling, weak tenure and access rights and increased climate variability. In the last 20 years, Somalia has lost almost 14 per cent of its forest cover, largely because of unregulated charcoal making.

Economic recovery was the second pillar in the Federal Government's Six Pillar Policy. The Government explicitly recognized that "more than two decades of conflict and state collapse have created an unregulated economy where livelihoods became so fragile and vulnerable, increasing an abject poverty that dehumanized the population". It therefore set the goal for economic reform "to create an enabling environment for investment, public and private, domestic and foreign, as a driver for sustainable and diversified and a solid economic growth and job creation."[66]

The 2013 New Deal Compact continued the emphasis in its PSG 4, dedicated to "revitalize and expand the Somali economy with a focus on livelihood enhancement, employment generation,

---

63   African Development Bank Group, Somalia country brief: 2013-2015 (2013).

64   USAID Somalia: Environmental and Natural Resource Management Assessment, April 2014.

65   Ibid.

66   http://www.villasomalia.gov.so/project/foundations-of-new-beginning-the-six-pillar-policy/

and broad-based inclusive growth." PSG 4 in turn has three priorities:

a) enhance the productivity of high-priority sectors and related value chains, including through the rehabilitation and expansion of critical infrastructure for transport, market access, trade and energy;

b) expand opportunities for youth employment through job creation and skills development;

c) promote the sustainable development and management of natural resources by developing legal and regulatory frameworks and building capacity in key natural resources management institutions.

The Federal Government's Economic Recovery Plan aims to provide the common vision and framework for coordination, together with the New Deal Compact which informed the plan's priorities. The Economic Recovery Plan is the instrument by which New Deal compact priorities for PSGs 4 (economic foundations) and 5 (revenue and services) are converted into costed programmes and implemented.

The UNDP strategy and how it developed

The CPD 2011-2015, the outcome paper and the poverty reduction and environmental protection programme document were all developed prior to the New Deal, and based on considerations and documents that now appear to be obsolete, such as the Somali Reconstruction and Development Programme (RDP) issued by the Transitional Federal Government in January 2008, itself based on a joint needs assessment conducted in 2005-2006. Similarly, the UNSAS is based on the RDP, and the question arises as to its relevance today, in that the goals pursued by these UNDP strategic documents are not aligned particularly well with those of the Compact and most importantly, use none of the recognizable New Deal language and programme structure.

While the 2013 and 2014 annual reports for UNDP Somalia present a credible picture of the country programme under new PSG headings, the PSG livelihoods goals (priorities 1 and 2 of PSG 4, economic foundations) are sharply focused on job training and job creation through infrastructure rehabilitation programmes, much more so than indicated in the UNDP documentation. PSG4 has a strong focus on value chains, trade and the private sector, but these are weakly articulated in the UNDP programme documents (CPD, outcome paper, poverty reduction and environmental protection project document). Only priority 3 of PSG 4 (Promote the sustainable development and management of natural resources by developing legal and regulatory frameworks and building capacity in key natural resources management institutions) is couched in language somewhat similar to the UNDP environment programme component as described in the CPD (sub-outcome 3.3) and outcome documents, in that it is just as vague as per the means of implementation nationwide of any new natural resources management policy initiative. However, even this priority area of the PSG is more context-specific than the UNDP documentation.

Components at the output level

The poverty reduction and environmental protection programme is the main framework of activities contributing to this outcome result area.[67] The **private sector development** project supported initiatives aimed at reducing poverty and hastening Somali economic recovery. It has supported respective ministries of planning to conduct public-private dialogues and baseline surveys for public-private partnerships in Somaliland, and to develop similar dialogues and partnership frameworks in Puntland. It revised and updated commercial and foreign investment laws and supported efforts to establish units that now collect, analyse and disseminate livestock information to local markets. The project has conducted training for approximately 1,350 youth in Mogadishu,

---

67 It also responds to two of the remaining CPD outcome areas: capacity-building for peace and human security, and gender equality.

  CHAPTER 4. THE UNDP CONTRIBUTION TO DEVELOPMENT RESULTS

Puntland and Somaliland. The project supported the creation of 200 micro-enterprises in Puntland and 200 in Somaliland. International trade represents a new area of work, which could potentially contribute to private sector development.[68] The project will assist Somalia to build trade competitiveness and integrate into global trade networks, including support to become a beneficiary country of the Enhanced Integrated Framework of the World Trade Organization.

The **local economic development** project combines two earlier projects[69] that supported: (a) recovery of Somali communities in regions affected by conflict, hazards, disasters and displacement; and (b) income generation and job creation through community-based approaches. Key outputs include the employment of up to 18,907 people in 2011[70] in various short-term rehabilitation projects of productive and basic social infrastructure (e.g., schools, health centres and markets). The project conducted diverse skills training for 2,326 people over 2011-2014. Two initiatives also strengthened the capacities of persons living with HIV/AIDS (120 people in Garowe and Bosaso) in business management and provided them with microgrants. Some 491 vulnerable youth (46 per cent women) received socioeconomic rehabilitation and reintegration support.

UNDP policy and programme development interventions in the **environmental management** area included a number of upstream interventions, including to: (a) draft a national environment policy and initiate a national environment action plan; (2) draft the United Nations joint programme for sustainable charcoal production and alternative livelihoods; (c) prepare cross-sectoral contingency plans for disaster management in Somaliland; (d) develop an inventory of greenhouse gas emissions in line with the United Nations Framework Convention on Climate Change; (e) initiate a national plan of action against desertification in line with the United Nations Convention to Combat Desertification; and (f) ensure that existing and newly developed sector plans incorporate disaster and environmental concerns. The project delivered medium-capacity solar energy systems to six large hospitals, benefiting around 80,000 patients each year. Flood protection works in Somaliland were supported under the disaster risk reduction initiative. Some 3,500 households in Karkaar (Puntland) were provided with energy efficient stoves and 1,700 households in Lower Juba were provided with solar cookers as an alternative source of energy.

FINDING: Given the size of the country, the national ambition of the programme, the top-heaviness of the programme cost structure, the high operational costs in Somalia and the fact that the poverty reduction and environment programme has had only modest success so far in attracting funding, UNDP interventions under the programme amount to a collection of small, on-off injections of assistance in various locales, which are neither cumulative nor transformative.

Beside the meetings held by the team itself with implementers and beneficiaries, the ADR can draw from a series of quarterly and annual activity reports, a recent evaluation of the local economic development project[71] and the study commissioned by the ADR team and undertaken by local data collectors. The quarterly and annual activity reports tend to focus on the output level and their outcome claims are often "optimistic". The local economic development evaluation report contains very scant information about outcomes and for some unknown reason

---

68 For example, moving from the export of live animals for the Gulf into meat packing, leather industries, etc.

69 Area-based early recovery for affected communities and employment generation for early recovery.

70 This number dropped thereafter to a total of 5,641 employed people in 2012; 3,860 in 2013 (42 per cent women); and 1,754 in 2014 (30 per cent women).

71 UNDP Somalia, Employment Generation for Early Recovery Project and Area-Based Early Recovery Project Evaluation Report, by Jean-Marc Bergevin & Aliou Diop for ADA CONSULTANTS Inc., June 2013.

covers only the federal level. The local data collectors were contracted precisely to compensate for the paucity of outcome information, and the report provides good independent insight into social dynamism around the rehabilitated infrastructures and trainings it sampled. It is therefore an important source of information for this chapter. This source however does not cover the policy and research work undertaken under the human development/Millennium Development Goal component. Predicting the outcome of the national human development report or of the National Environment Policy would be difficult at this stage, other than to say that the former leads to recommendations that are useful although not profound, and that UNDP has been active in ensuring that the environmental sector as a whole, and the climate change response plan in particular, be included in the New Deal Compact and Economic Recovery Plan, which means that the implementation of these plans could receive further funding.

Most of the field-level interventions reviewed appeared useful at several levels (societal, economic, security-wise, etc.) and were strongly supported by a wide variety of interviewed beneficiaries. The general message from these beneficiaries, however, is that this assistance is good but not widespread enough and often provided on an ad hoc, intermittent basis. The overall picture therefore is one of interesting and useful work, but which is undertaken at too small a scale.

As it currently stands, the UNDP support in the sustainable livelihoods outcome is much too small in scope to respond to actual needs. In Puntland, for instance, the poverty reduction and environment programme has helped to rehabilitate a total of 6.2 kilometres, out of a total of 1,151 kilometres, of registered gravel surfaced feeder roads in the state.[72] The work is of good quality but pales in comparison with the needs. According to the Puntland Highway Authority,

developing a better road network has a strategic importance for the state, not only for security reasons but also because currently many people are resettling along the Galkayo – Garowe – Bosaso axis (the only hard-top road in the state) to benefit from services such as hospitals or banks which exist only along the tarmac. 'Remote communities' (including large towns along the Indian Ocean coast, such as Bandar Beyla or Eyl) need better access so that services can develop there too.

The same applies to the job creation programme. PSG 4 forecasts the creation of 250,000 short-term jobs, while the UNDP employment generation for early recovery and other projects report a total of 28,000 short-term jobs created over the past four years, and 61,000 jobs from 2008 to 2012, according to the local economic development evaluation. Clearly UNDP is capable of delivering relevant projects in this area, but its interventions cover only a small fraction of the needs.

Similarly, vocational training appears to be in high demand. In the local economic development evaluation, one learns that 30 per cent of respondents who followed a vocational training course have secured a job and a further 33 per cent have "acquired a skill-related attachment". This seems to translate into improved earnings, logically enough.

The ADR team also met with many satisfied beneficiaries. Often the most recent trainings were undertaken together with the community security project under outcome 1, and officially targeted 'youth at risk', i.e., ex-thieves and pirates. In practice, most of them are simply school dropouts and jobless youth. This in itself is not a problem. Joblessness can lead to social wrongs and petty crime. However, the social rehabilitation part of the training (6 months out of a total of 9 months, in some cases) was wasted on them.

---

72 This modest tally, based on the Somali Joint Needs Assessment Infrastructure Cluster Report, September 2006 (http://www.somali-jna.org/downloads/SJNAICR090906%20-%20Infrust%20Part%20I.pdf), supposedly exclude numerous tracks built by communities themselves.

CHAPTER 4. THE UNDP CONTRIBUTION TO DEVELOPMENT RESULTS

What they really want is the vocational training and cash injection.

The report of the local data collectors confirmed this diagnostic. It covered six project sites concerned with vocational training and aimed at providing alternative livelihoods to piracy and gainful employment to potential and actual perpetrators of violence, all located in the southern and central regions and Puntland:

a) Galkayo Vocational Training Centre;

b) Vocational skills training in Adado District;

c) 'Youth for Change'[73] Eyl Business Services Development Centre;

d) Three resource centres for peace managed by Aamin Voluntary and Relief Organization (AVRO), Centre for Peace and Democracy and Somali Youth Development Network (SOYDEN) in Wadajir, Hamar Jajab and Karan districts of Banadir Region (near Mogadishu).

It appears from these sites that the beneficiaries were rarely youth 'at risk' of piracy or petty thievery. Rather, most seem to be jobless or underemployed youths. Their demands are typically related to the need for a lengthier and more advanced technical training programme, as one would expect from people with an interest in vocational training. This suggests the need to de-emphasize the social rehabilitation part of the training and strengthen the technical courses.

Another general issue in some of those vocational training projects lies in the kits or moneys intended to be donated to the students at the end of each training session to help them launch their business. The kits have repeatedly not been made available to the students, or in lesser quantities than originally promised. In some cases, this seems to be the result of fraud by the implementing institution.[74] In other cases, poor collaboration with another United Nations organization was faulted. This issue has in some cases led to severe disputes, e.g., in the Galkayo Vocational Training Centre, and requires systematic monitoring to uphold the rights of beneficiary students and protect the reputation of UNDP among the general community, local authorities and donors.

The support to the development of a regulatory framework for microfinance and to microfinance institutions seems to be on and off, without a strong 'champion' among programme staff. As a result, it is still unclear from the recently produced draft microfinance policies and strategies how the country would build a microfinance industry that is institutionally and financially sustainable, and integrated within a viable, well-regulated formal financial sector. The UNDP work on the different Islamic finance modalities available and how they can be used for microfinance (including for saving services), initiated with an excellent study at the Federal level[75] and workshops in Puntland and Somaliland in 2013, has not been followed up. There is no clear lending/microcredit strategy and, in particular, no repayment strategy in the current poverty reduction and environmental protection projects in support of women's groups, persons living with AIDS, etc. whom the programme supports through modest cash injections. These are handed out by NGOs partnering with the programme against vague promises of repayment. This lax approach runs the risk of worsening the local credit repayment culture. These projects do not work with specialized microfinance partners and have too short a duration (6 to 12 months each) to allow for the building of any sustainable microfinance capacity.

The poverty reduction and environment programme also constructed or rehabilitated market

---

73 A project within the peace and security cluster discussed in more detail in the next section.

74 E.g., the provision of business skills training and microgrants to 400 'youth at risk' in Galdogob district, Mudug region in 2012-2013, currently under investigation.

75 UNDP Somalia, 'Institutionalizing Islamic Finance in South Central Somalia', by Abubakr I. M. Hussein, March 2013.

shelters, including a meat and vegetable market and a fish market with ice-making facilities in Garowe; the rehabilitation and expansion of the Galkayo market; and an expansion of the general market in Bosaso. These market projects appear popular with the respective mayors and local authorities, probably because they potentially enhance the capacity of the local authority or municipality to collect revenue through rent fees from the market users. For instance, in Adado District, the expansion of the existing market responded to a demand by the city council. The newly built and rehabilitated markets are used and, according to the local authorities, have already generated additional taxation revenue.[76]

For the same reasons, the rehabilitation and extension of the Bosaso food market was a strong priority of the Bosaso mayor, who contributed $15,000 to its cost from the Bosaso Authority's own budget. The previous market burned down in 2012 and many vendors were operating on the streets. The new building, located at the centre of the town, has several floors instead of just one like the previous market, but the second and third floors currently are not occupied. The vendors who are supposed to move there (vegetable and meat vendors) refuse to occupy them and demand space on the first floor, now occupied by milk vendors. Some of the interviewees believed it was a poor choice to build a multi-story market for vendors who are accustomed to working on the streets where customer visibility is high. They believe customers will not come to them if they are trading on the second or third floor of the new market. This case highlights a weakness in many poverty reduction and environmental protection projects: the lack of a prolonged engagement with the local community during project design. In most reviewed cases, this did not pose a major problem as the projects were simple enough and the local authorities (council, mayor) had a sufficient grasp of the issues. But in the more complex case of the Bosaso market, a lack

of community consultation became a stumbling block. A committee comprised of community leaders, business people and the local government should have been established immediately to prepare the market design and plan for management arrangements. This was mentioned in the project document but it does not appear that such a committee was ever established.

In the Somali context, the revenues generated by a thriving market can attract attention from many more people than just the local legal authorities. In Galkayo for instance, the programme responded to the local mayor's demand to rehabilitate the city's marketplace. Construction was successfully completed in 2014 but the site is currently occupied by a local armed group demanding compensation for 'protection' of the land upon which the market sits. The local authority of Galkayo has already paid some money, but they have asked for more.

The rehabilitated vegetable and meat market in downtown Garowe is a women-managed affair which operates well. The Garowe fish market, situated right next to the vegetable and meat market, was supposed to be managed by a similar group of women, according to programme staff, but was handed over by the Puntland Ministry of Fisheries to a rich businessman instead, who has since declined to meet with UNDP.[77] From a site visit, it appears that the ice-making facility is being used to sell ice to restaurants in Garowe, and that the stalls are only occasionally supplied with fish coming from the coast. This facility is operating well under its full capacity.

Another fisheries project in Berbera (the 'Berbera Fish Project') was visited by the beneficiary assessment team but the contact person in Berbera was uncooperative and could not escort the team, provide access to the project site or identify specific beneficiaries. Interviewed fishermen talked of some sort of mismanagement.

---

76 Part of the tax collected is reportedly used for operational and maintenance of the market, which is registered as a public property that the Government must support.

77 He also declined to meet the evaluation mission.

It should be stressed that fisheries projects tend to involve significant assets, necessarily donated to private concerns, and they therefore frequently end up controlled by the economic elite in their areas of operation.[78]

The only project that comes across as significant in scope is the solar panel systems provided to hospitals in Burao, Garowe and two other locations. In both Burao and Garowe, the directors of the hospitals reported that the solar installations (large tents which can be used for storage) worked well and had reduced the hospitals' electricity costs by several thousand dollars a month. The money saved as a result of the project is reportedly used for other vital operations including medical supplies. These hospitals are the primary medical facilities in Togdheer Region and Puntland, respectively, and treat hundreds of patients a day. Thus they are vital to a wide community.

4.1.2 INCLUSIVE, EQUITABLE AND ACCOUNTABLE GOVERNANCE

> **Planned outcome result:** Somali women and men, girls and boys, benefit from more inclusive, equitable and accountable governance, improved services, human security, access to justice and human rights.

Overview

As described in chapter 2, since 2011 Somalia has undergone major governance reforms and Somalis are establishing a governance framework that is more representative and transparent than at any time during the 20 years. Notably, the establishment of the National Constituent Assembly and the adoption of the Provisional Federal Constitution paved the way for the formation of a new Parliament, the selection of a Speaker of Parliament and the selection of a President. Once consolidated, the new federal framework established by the Provisional Constitution has the potential to further promote representation and inclusivity.

The Federal Government's Six Pillar Strategy addressed inclusive, equitable and accountable governance through the first pillar, the purpose of which is to "establish legitimacy and the authority of the State of one Country, and on a Vision whereby the citizens become capable of maintaining their basic needs and trust their Government's ability to deliver lasting peace and progress". It also recognizes that "absence of the rule of law undermines the Legitimacy of the State." Equally important and with similar planning objectives, good governance and public finance management aim to deter corruption at all levels of government, rebuild the country and restore people's trust and confidence in governance systems and the rule of law.

Work in this area relates to PSGs 1 and 3. The strategic objective of PSG 1 (Inclusive Politics) is to "Achieve a stable and peaceful federal Somalia through inclusive political processes". It sets out three priorities:

a) advance inclusive political dialogue to clarify and settle relations between the Federal Government and existing and emerging administrations and initiate processes of social reconciliation to restore trust between communities;

b) finalize and adopt a Federal Constitution by December 2015;

c) prepare for and hold credible elections by 2016.

The outcome is also aligned with PSG 3 (Justice) with the strategic objective to "Establish independent and accountable justice institutions capable of addressing the justice needs of the people of Somalia by delivering justice for all." It also sets out three priorities:

a) key priority laws in the legal framework, including on the reorganization of the judi-

---

78 See for instance, Real-Time Evaluation of the FAO Emergency and Rehabilitation Operations in Response to the Indian Ocean Earthquake and Tsunami, April 2007.

ciary, are aligned with the Constitution and international standards;

b) justice institutions start to address the key grievances and injustices of Somalis;

c) more Somalis have access to fair and affordable justice.

The UNDP strategy and how it developed

The strategy developed over time, as have the programming and other documents that frame it. Noting that transitional governance and rule of law institutions within Somalia are very fragile, the CPD committed UNDP to strengthening governance and rule of law institutions, systems, practices and services. The 'outcome implementation guide' stated that the focus of this outcome will be interventions working in partnership with authorities and civil society to:

a) ensure inclusive political settlements and processes;

b) develop core state functions and accountability mechanisms focusing on community security and safety and access to justice within the framework of the rule of law;

c) ensure that they respond to public expectations, including the provision of basic services.

As noted in the previous chapter, changes in context and lessons learned from the ongoing work of UNDP led to the development of the governance and rule of law programme in 2012, merging the previously stand-alone programmes for governance and rule of law and for security. The new programme aimed to enhance the quality and impact of UNDP work across Somalia through thematically interlinked focus areas.

Components at the output level

The UNDP **access to justice** project operates at the policy level to help develop frameworks and strategies to guide the development of the justice sector. In Somaliland, the judicial reform strategy, developed with UNDP support, lays the foundation for an accountable, functioning and accessible judiciary and court system. In early 2011, Puntland approved the code of conduct regulating the judiciary, Attorney General's office and legal profession, which is the first such provision in Somalia providing a framework for accountability for justice actors. The project also aimed to increase the number of qualified lawyers, court staff and judges through capacity-building, scholarships in legal education and internships in the public sector (half of them for women). For example, the Somaliland regional government recruited 15 female lawyers in 2013 after they completed a UNDP-supported one-year legal internship programme, and a total of 52 women who completed UNDP-supported graduate internships are now serving in various positions in the justice sector.

UNDP raised awareness about the judiciary and the rule of law through support to law faculties, legal centres and law students. CSOs supported by UNDP trained members of civil society in Somaliland and Puntland to promote effective responses and consistent reporting on sexual and gender-based violence. Awareness-raising was complemented with legal aid to over 40,000 people at the community level through support to universities, NGOs and mobile courts and paralegals. UNDP-supported mobile courts, designed to reach people in rural and hard-to-access locations, heard 3,569 cases in 2013 and 2014. The project also partnered with other UNDP initiatives such as: (a) the civilian police project to integrate legal studies as part of training for criminal investigators; and (b) the community security project[79] to support the prosecutor's office to select youth offenders to participate in alternative sentencing. Gender has been mainstreamed into this area through 'women and children desks' in the Hargeisa Group Hospital supporting survivors of sexual violence, and a Puntland women's organization's judicial monitoring tool to facilitate systematic and consistent data collection on cases of sexual and gender-based violence.

---

79 Formerly the Armed Violence Reduction Project, described in the next section.

Support to the new Constitution, formerly implemented by the Joint Constitution Unit (JCU) with UNPOS, aimed to help develop a Constitution, better governance systems and a process that builds peace and reconciliation among Somali constituents through public consultation and civic education. As the lead agency for good governance and co-leader with UNPOS of the constitutional benchmark process, UNDP was an active stakeholder in the transitional road map. The JCU assisted in convening the first National Constitutional Conference (Garowe, Puntland, December 2011), which outlined the Garowe Principles directing the finalization of the Constitution. With technical assistance from UNDP, the Independent Federal Constitution Commission increased public consultations with citizens and CSOs on the draft Constitution document and process. Collaboration with UNPOS and other partners included finalizing the Provisional Federal Constitution approved by the National Constituent Assembly on 1 August 2012 and supporting the Assembly's convening under extremely difficult political and security conditions. This was a significant step towards achieving the tasks specified in the road map to the end the transition. The project further collaborated with the United Nations Support Office for the African Union Mission in Somalia and United Nations Mine Action Service in Somalia on security and provision of equipment to the Assembly.

UNDP has provided advice on legislation to the Independent Electoral Commission, established in October 2014, while setting up the integrated United Nations electoral assistance team together with UNSOM. UNDP provided the initial support to the team, which advised the Special Representative of the Secretary-General and the Government on election-related planning. UNDP also supported the 2013 Jubbaland Reconciliation Conference, which set up an Interim Jubba Administration. These bodies will have advisory functions and help the new Government to build democratic, sustainable and transparent foundations. As a result of the technical and financial support of the United Nations integrated team, a Policy and Legislative Drafting Unit was established in the Ministry of Justice and Constitutional Affairs in 2014, which in turn resulted in the passage of two acts. UNDP helped to strengthen the Parliament Secretariat through the UNDP Young Graduates Initiative. Some 45 graduates (including five women) were placed with the Parliament. Parliamentary committees (15 in the Federal Parliament and eight in the Somaliland Parliament) were strengthened and supported to conduct debates, regional visits, oversight missions and review meetings. The UNDP 'support to Parliament project' has been integral to the New Deal process and was supposed to help achieve ratification of a new permanent Constitution by the end of 2015.

Support to government capacity development was implemented through the Somali Institutional Develop Project (SIDP)[80] to strengthen key central government and public institutions at Federal level Somalia, Puntland and Somaliland for more effective public service delivery. The three governments faced common challenges that explain the varying degrees of success of the project in supporting reform. UNDP addressed capacity gaps in human resources through, inter alia, civil service professionalization and management. UNDP supported a process of facilitating the Somali diaspora's transfer of core skills and technical capacity to staff in partner institutions.[81] In the area of public financial management, SIDP contributed to higher compliance with tax regulations by supporting

---

80 SIDP was formed from the merging of a number of related projects in mid-2008 in accordance with the Reconstruction and Development Programme so as to give a greater cohesion to a number of activities that tended towards a single objective: Somali Institutional Capacity Development Project; Qualified Somali Technical Support Project; Emergency Technical Assistance Project; Start-up Package Project; and Somalia Institutional Support Project.

81 The Qualified Expatriate Somali Technical Support - Migration for Development in Africa project, implemented with the International Organization for Migration, recruited 66 technical advisers across all three regions of Somalia.

a public awareness campaign that explained the role of government in providing public services and the responsibilities of citizens to pay taxes. UNDP continued supporting efforts to improve development effectiveness and aid management through the provision of the Development Assistance Database, a tool the Government can use to access development finance information on aid provided by the donor community.

The joint programme on local governance aimed to support good governance (transparency, accountability and participation) and enhance effective and efficient public management in regional/ district councils. It works with four other United Nations agencies – the United Nations Human Settlements Programme (UN-Habitat), United Nations Children's Fund (UNICEF), International Labour Organization (ILO) and the United Nations Capital Development Fund (UNCDF) – in Somaliland, Puntland and the Federal Government. Phase II (2013-2017) builds on the successes of the first phase (2008-2012) and seeks to support Somalia to expand decentralized service delivery through: (a) strengthening policy and legislative frameworks; (b) developing the capacities of local government and; (c) improving decentralized service delivery. The programme also supported the finalization of public expenditure management policies and managed related training to district and Ministry of Interior staff.

UNDP provided support to enhance the capacity of districts and Ministries of Interior to implement decentralization, including the establishment, mentoring, monitoring and evaluation of district councils. UNDP work in the area of local governance enabled the Offices of the Auditor General in Somaliland and Puntland to audit the districts, a precondition for allocation of local development funds. UNDP directly supported 13 district councils to effectively manage funds and respond to citizen demands, which resulted in improved access to basic services for 140,000 people. UNDP supported a change management process to improve effectiveness of the Municipality of Mogadishu and its coordination with the Federal Government of Somalia. UNDP provided technical support for producing a draft decentralization policy and road map for Somaliland and Puntland, which will be implemented in conjunction with a capacity development strategy. UNDP also supported the Ministry of Women's Development and Family Affairs and Ministry of Labor and Social Affairs in advocating gender equality in district councils and district administrations, and increased women's engagement in the local government political process and in processes for planning and implementing service delivery.[82]

FINDING: The level of effectiveness varies across the programme components. The joint programme on local governance, access to justice and Constitution projects generally have been more effective in helping to strengthen governance and rule of law institutions and are being expanded by authorities in some areas. On the other hand, SIDP only partially achieved its planned result of strengthened national capacities.

The joint programme on local governance has made a very important contribution to local governance in and potentially beyond the area in which it works. The joint programme appears to be a very effective intervention that exhibits great promise for contributing further to Somalia's future development goals. The UNDP 2014 annual report on the joint programme notes that a study in Somaliland's Burao district, conducted by the Observatory on Conflict and Violence Prevention, found that the number of people who knew who their local council representatives were had increased from 45 to 99 per cent in two years.

---

82   Ten women were elected (representing 2.6 per cent) as local councilors in Somaliland during the November 2012 local elections. As of December 2011, there were 44 women councilors in Puntland (representing 17.5 per cent). Of the 16 District Commissioners in the Benadir Region in Mogadishu, one is female.

The international community has a very positive view of the joint programme's effectiveness. A 2012 European Union assessment[83] found that "Despite the risks of agency rivalry and the potential blurring of oversight in such joint programmes, the [joint programme's] results have been impressive. The programme is appreciated by donors, particularly because of its transparent dialogue arrangements with donors and partner institutions and its elaborate monitoring and reporting practices". The report of a more recent joint donor monitoring mission[84] is equally positive: "Donors applaud and congratulate [the joint programme's] work on the ground in the difficult and fragile context of Somalia. There is strong evidence of results on policy and service delivery outcomes. Results on capacity building appear mixed. [The joint programme] needs to continue to improve on reporting so that the positive reality in the field is also reflected on paper." Such sentiments were also reflected by donor representative interviewed by the ADR team.

Government counterparts are generally happy with the joint programme and while donor plaudits are gratifying, a more important indicator of success is the willingness of the respective governments to replicate and expand the process, as is the case in Somaliland. One factor that can explain the success of the joint programme is its strong national ownership. The project appears to go beyond limited engagement (i.e., preparing interventions 'in consultation with') to genuine ownership at the local level.

In contrast, the recent evaluation of SIDP noted that although the project's aim was to develop national capacity, a majority of deliverables were focused on capacity substitution: "Instead of developing national capacities, short-term consultants, external experts were provided to the line Ministries who have done their work without fully engaging the government staff in the process. This led to non-institutionalisation of capacity and substituting the capacity".

The evaluation also criticized the practices of topping up salaries, providing operational expenditures and paying stipends to interns. The 'Qualified Expatriate Somali Technical Support - Migration for Development in Africa' project support system was seen as an expensive option by government officials in all regions. An earlier evaluation of SIDP commissioned by the European Union considered these practices more of a burden than a help.

The main objective of UNDP support to the constitutional process was to help Somalia move peacefully from the post-conflict situation and lay the foundation for stability and security. Between 2009 and 2012, UNDP played a long-term supporting role in the drafting and public consultation processes. It contributed significantly to the operational aspects of the National Constituent Assembly convened to provisionally adopt the Constitution. This intervention was always going to be highly risky, with much outside the control of UNDP, and the project was quite controversial. For example, the original Charter had envisaged a Constitution ratified by popular referendum in 2012 but this did not happen. Moreover, it is unclear if the project managed to increase the legitimacy of the constitutional process among ordinary Somalis through the UNDP-supported Committee of Experts.[85] A recent report on NORAD support to UNDP in Somalia concluded that UNDP handling of the project must be said to have been relatively successful under the circumstances, working against heavy odds.

Senior officials in the Ministry of Justice in Somaliland expressed satisfaction with UNDP

---

83 Development Note EU Somalia Unit September 2011–May 2012.

84 Source: Joint Donor Monitoring Mission, February 2014.

85 Ainte, A, 'Legitimacy of the Provisional Constitution'. Accord, Issue 25. See also Kouroutakis, A, 'The Provisional Constitution of Somalia: Process, Architecture and Perspectives', Journal of International and Comparative Law.

support though access to justice, noting that people are more satisfied with the new judges and lawyers. This is notwithstanding some cooperation issues related to the use of letters of agreement that are discussed further in chapter 5. Through the project, over 75 women are working in the legal sector in Somaliland compared to fewer than five in 2008.[86] Legal aid appears to have been very successful in reaching the marginalized in spite of the need to clarify the roles of the respective Ministries of Justice with the legal aid providers. A recent evaluation of the mobile courts in Somaliland[87] noted the excellent synergy with other elements of UNDP access to justice work. It also noted the good cooperation with the traditional Xeer system[88] that often represents a challenge to the formal justice system. The project recognized the key role played by elders in supporting the mobile court system and established informal linkages between elders and the mobile courts. Specifically, elders refer cases, contribute to the enforcement of mobile court decisions, provide information about the courts to communities and occasionally ensure that perpetrators are brought before the courts.

> **Planned outcome result:** Somali women and men and authorities are better able to build peace and manage conflict.

Overview

It has already been noted that Somalia is coming out of a period of insecurity and that insecurity remains. During the ADR review period, Somalia experienced a major increase in violence, with peak periods in July 2013 and July 2014. Clearly the risk of increased insecurity remains. In Somalia, over 70 per cent of the population is under the age of 30 and the youth unemployment rate is 67 per cent, one of the highest rates in the world. Youth are thus at risk of becoming involved in crime or terrorism.

Building peace and addressing security issues are therefore essential for economic, social and political development. Peacebuilding was at the core of the initial manifesto of the Federal Government of Somalia, the Six Pillar Policy, with the explicit goal to "provide safety and security to all Somali citizens, protecting Somali sovereignty and thereby contributing towards national and regional stability". The policy also recognized that to achieve this goal will require "de-politicized, impartial, accountable, transparent, and professional security forces, including the military and police". The Somali Compact specifically designed the five PSGs to represent agreement on what is required to move towards peace and recovery.

As also noted in chapter 2, the African Union and United Nations are providing major support through AMISOM and UNSOM. The AMISOM police component has the mandate to train, mentor, monitor and advise the Somali Police Force with the aim of transforming it into a credible and effective organization adhering to strict international standards. In addition, a number of donors have provided support to the security sector and at the 2013 New Deal conference agreed to scale up their support for reinforcing the Somali security forces.

The UNDP strategy and how it developed

In describing this component, the CPD noted that "the overarching objective of the country programme document is dedicated to the building of capacities for peace and human security". It set out the following components:

a) UNDP will diversify its participation in strategic peacebuilding activities, such as the consti-

---

86 UNDP Somalia website.

87 Rispo, Monica, 'Evaluation of UNDP-supported mobile courts interventions in Somaliland, Sierra Leone and Democratic Republic of Congo. Somaliland County Study', UNDP Bureau of Crisis Prevention and Recovery, New York, 2013.

88 A customary legal system where elders serve as judges and help mediate cases using precedents.

tutional process, including CSOs, particularly women's groups and the private sector, to deepen peace within their own communities;

b) UNDP will strengthen its analytical capabilities and help strengthen the capacity of its partners to better analyse and manage conflict;

c) UNDP will also seek to promote more regional and inter-zonal cooperation. Human Development Reports will research human security, community safety and human rights, featuring issues such as youth inclusion, gender inequality, women's empowerment, community cohesion and integrated peace and development initiatives.

UNDP will apply its capacity development framework to ensure that a consistent approach is applied at all levels. The governance and rule of law programme described in the previous chapter included two elements directly related to this outcome: (a) strengthening police and security sector governance; and (b) enhancing community security and resilience. A strong police force must emphasize community security and have linkages with those mechanisms. This means empowering communities to use tools to target their unique challenges and environments.

These direct interventions were to be supported by a strategy to mainstream peacebuilding across all UNDP work in Somalia, working towards creating an environment of increased peace and stability by supporting institutions, civil society and communities to manage conflict peacefully. UNDP aspires to build the capacity of Somali men and women to manage conflict and build peace through all its programming.

In 2012, UNDP developed a peacebuilding support strategy to guide its work that it described as "programming through a peacebuilding lens". This was defined as "tailoring traditional UNDP thematic programmes in the areas of democratic governance, poverty reduction and [Millennium Development Goal] achievement, energy and the environment, and crisis prevention and recovery, so that they address the key drivers of conflict and help establish the foundations for sustainable peace." To this end, throughout 2012 the country office reviewed its programmes from a peace and conflict perspective, developing fresh approaches that allowed each project to maximise its peacebuilding impact and ensure it was doing no harm. To implement this mainstreaming approach, the strategy proposed the establishment of a peacebuilding unit in the country office. While the unit was not established, the mainstreaming approach was maintained.

As described in the previous chapter, the UNDP approach was to develop broad programme documents for each of the four outcomes. The design of the three-year programme, 'towards a just and sustainable peace in Somalia', was completed in early 2013 with an aspirational budget of nearly $7 million. The programme was not approved but the mainstreaming principle was continued and by the time of the ADR in early 2014, the two security areas were considered to be the main efforts towards achieving the outcome.

In September 2012, the Secretary-General designated the Department of Peacekeeping Operations (DPKO) and UNDP as the global focal point for the police, justice and corrections areas in the rule of law in post-conflict and other crisis situations. Drawing upon a past history of collaboration, the overall aim of the global focal point arrangement is to respond more quickly and effectively to rule of law needs in post-conflict societies and societies in crisis. Under this mechanism, UNDP and DPKO, as cluster leads, bring all relevant United Nations actors together to plan, support and deliver rule of law results.

Components at the output level

The two main components directly contributing to the planned outcome are UNDP work with: (a) civilian police; and (b) community security. UNDP also provided advisory support to the Ministries of Security and Interior in Puntland and Somaliland on related issues, and prepared a human development report focused on youth that received the 2013 Human Development Award for Excellence.[89] The **civilian police** component aims to support the development of a police force that is more responsive to the security needs of communities. The project worked with law enforcement personnel to ensure that they are properly equipped to protect citizens, especially in violent and insecure areas, including through support payment systems, materials, and infrastructure rehabilitation. Some 12,000 police have graduated the three-month basic police training since 2008. The project also supported development policy frameworks, including police acts in Somaliland and at federal level. The Ministry of Interior and the Somali Police Force implemented a security plan for the National Constituent Assembly and national elections with UNDP support. UNDP additionally focused on capacity development for key institutions that deliver civilian policing, including public accountability and parliamentary oversight mechanisms. Model police stations were developed in 2012 to ensure that policing responds to the needs of the community.[90] The project has mainstreamed gender issues, evidenced inter alia by the 2013 Action Plan for Gender-Responsive Policing in Somaliland, training of women officers and a piloted Women's Civilian Protection Unit.

The **community security** component is built around three key areas: (a) the infrastructure of peace; (b) information for evidence-based policy-making; and (c) addressing specific issues related to youth. In the first area, UNDP supported the establishment of peacebuilding units in Puntland, Somaliland and Mogadishu to develop roles, responsibilities and partnerships among authorities at all levels. The project supported governments to formalize a common framework under a Community Security and Peacebuilding Policy in Puntland to institutionalize partnerships between state actors and civil society. District safety committees established in all regions aimed to empower communities to monitor and reduce violence. In the second area, the project conducted community-level safety and security assessments in five districts and supported the Observatory of Conflict and Violence Prevention to pilot a monitoring framework and conduct field research. UNDP equally supported an evidence-based programme design tool with the United Nations Institute for Disarmament Research for use by reintegration practitioners.[91] In the third area, UNDP worked with UNICEF and ILO to steer at-risk youth away from criminal activities (e.g., piracy and armed violence). Youth at risk organized a social rehabilitation programme for youth that was complemented by economic reintegration activities. A second phase called 'Youth for Change' targeted social rehabilitation activities, including training 491 youth on a wide range of skills and topics in 2014.

FINDING: While UNDP support under the civilian police and community security projects has contributed to improved capacities at individual and institutional levels, programme design and targeting-related issues can be improved to enhance effectiveness.

UNDP has contributed to the outcome in both areas of intervention and through the cross-cutting work with other programmes. It is clear that at such an early stage of development of the civilian police force, UNDP support to basic individual and institutional capacity development has been important. There seem to have been lost opportunities due to poor strategy in the area of protection of women through the women's and children's desks at police stations. The civilian police proj-

---

89 The awards programme seeks to recognize publicly the contributions of regional, national and local Human Development Reports in stimulating development dialogue and policy formulation influenced by the human development concept and approach in countries and regions. The ADR team noted that this report is widely quoted and used in analysis of the situation in Somalia.

90 By 2014, two model police stations had been constructed in Somaliland and three in Puntland.

91 Miller, Derek B. and Lisa Rudnick, 'A Prototype for Evidence-Based Programme Design for Reintegration, United Nations Institute for Disarmament Research'. The report notes that the Observatory for Conflict and Violence Prevention at the University of Hargeysa, Somaliland, provided support, insight and valuable cooperation in the prototype's testing.

ect conducted a study on these desks at Somaliland police stations which revealed that women beneficiaries became further marginalized from receiving assistance from the police, because the desks were not sufficiently incorporated into the overall structure of the police stations. The officers trained for those functions had been deployed elsewhere. Effective women's and children's desks are often staffed exclusively by women police personnel or women and men especially trained to deal with victims of sexual crimes and to build effective investigations. The desks help to counter the underreporting of crimes against women that are ubiquitous in patriarchal societies as well as in their police services.

The successful implementation of the joint 'youth at risk' programme demonstrated that an alternative to the usual disarmament, demobilization and reintegration approach can be implemented in countries facing high levels of violence, organized crime and conflict such as Somalia. Evidence collected on the 'youth for change' project[92] in southern and central regions and Puntland indicates that the project appears to have made a significant contribution to some of the primary desired outcomes, including social rehabilitation and improving literacy skills. The instructors interviewed in the southern and central regions reported that they had seen a vast difference in many of the beneficiaries' behaviour post-project induction, with higher levels of discipline and self-conduct. Some of the parents interviewed in the same places reported that prior to the training their children sympathized with Al-Shabaab, but were now moving away from adopting an extremist ideology. Many of the beneficiaries reported that the lessons provided through the Resource Centres for Peace were effective and they were now able to read and write, having been previously illiterate.

Some of the youth were able to demonstrate their new abilities in the presence of the data collectors. A measure was put in place that would immediately replace any youth who dropped out. According to the project staff, as a result, the beneficiaries were incentivized to stay in the programme and considered themselves lucky to have been given the opportunity. The beneficiary selection criteria appeared suitable and well thought through, with special attention given to minorities who were often targeted by Al-Shabaab in order to exploit their grievances with dominant clans. There remains, however, an issue (already raised in section 4.1) as to the degree to which participants are 'at risk' and if the programme is really targeting the intended beneficiaries.

Several other issues were reported to impact the overall effectiveness of the project. In each Resource Centre for Peace, the beneficiaries were divided into only two classes, due to limited resources for procuring additional instruction space. This hindered the learning process as many of the students had different levels of competency. According to the project staff, they requested additional funds from UNDP to increase both the number of classes and the overall number of beneficiaries. The 'youth for change' management suggested increasing the number of youth beneficiaries from 65 to 200 per district because the number proposed by UNDP was nowhere near sufficient and the project would be less effective. The project staff at all three district sites visited were able to provide some documentation showing the number of beneficiaries served. They all appear to be on track to meet their target numbers.

4.1.4 GENDER EQUALITY AND WOMEN'S EMPOWERMENT

> **Planned outcome result:** Somali women and men attain greater gender equality and are empowered.

Overview

There have been some notable positive changes in the constitutional process and policies with the new 2012 Provisional Constitution of the Federal

---

92 According to collected documents, observations made by the data collectors and interviews at the Resource Centres for Peace in Wadajir, Hamar Jajab and Karan Districts.

Republic of Somalia, under the general principles of human rights and articulating provisions prohibiting discrimination across numerous categories, including on the basis on gender. Principles of gender equity and women's rights are enshrined in the individual constitutions of Somaliland and Puntland. Notably absent from all three constitutions, however, is language providing for a 30 per cent quota for women in representative bodies of government, for which political and women's rights organizations had vigorously advocated and which had appeared in earlier drafts. The 30 per cent allotment had been earlier enshrined within the 'Garowe II Principles,' an agreement signed in February 2012 which set forth the new institutional structures to replace the Transitional Government.[93] In Somaliland, the proposal from women's groups has been volleyed back and forth between the President and Parliament.

Although gender policies and strategies have been developed, their adoption and implementation have been slow. The Federal Government of Somalia has a draft gender policy that was developed in 2013 with the assistance of AMISOM. In Puntland, a draft gender policy continues to be met with resistance from the Cabinet, Parliament and religious leaders and still has not been adopted. Puntland's five-year development strategy (2012-2016),[94] created by the Ministry of Planning, appears to be gender-sensitive, although implementation thus far shows little evidence of that sensitivity.

Somaliland adopted a comprehensive national gender policy in 2009 under the Ministry of Family Affairs and Social Development which recognized women's empowerment at all levels of the clan, community and society. It recommended specifically the elimination of gender inequalities and women's access to equitable development.

The gender policy has an implementation plan which was the subject of consultations with various ministries and CSOs. An interministerial coordination mechanism on gender has been established, with focal points appointed from 13 ministries and from local CSOs. According to key informants interviewed, there does not appear to be any initiative or budget to support policy implementation.[95]

Bilateral donors expect UNDP to address gender and human rights in its programmes. Donors such as the United Kingdom, Denmark, Sweden and Norway have supported gender activities by channelling dedicated funds through United Nations partners or other implementing organizations. Some bilateral donors support programmes that might have some impact on gender issues but the funding has not necessarily been targeted to promote gender-specific outcomes.[96] Denmark is a major bilateral donor to UNDP for gender equality programming. Sweden is the main bilateral donor through UN-Women. The European Union and USAID have documented the gender situation through gender audits[97] and assessments covering all of the country. Norway and Sweden have also provided lessons learned through various broad evaluations of their work in Somalia. Coordination among bilateral donors is weak in the area of gender equality but strong on human rights. Bilateral donors are considering merging coordination for the two aspects. Within the New Deal Compact, although gender is a cross-cutting area within the PSGs, there are no specific gender priorities for each PSG and gender is totally absent from the PSG results matrix.

Following the signing of the New Deal Compact, UNDP Somalia took steps to align its ongoing programmes with the five PSGs. Gender equality and women's empowerment cut across all five

---

93   'Learning on gender and conflict in Africa: gender and conflict note, Somalia', March 2013.

94   Puntland's Five Year Development Strategy (2012-2016).

95   UNDP, 2013, Gender in Somalia, Brief II.

96   Discussion with donors and 'Learning on gender and conflict in Africa: gender and conflict note, Somalia', March 2013.

97   See European Union, Gender Audit Report, 2013.

goals. Specific benchmarks or expected results are not spelled out under each PSG. The role and responsibility of the Ministry of Women and Human Rights is not contemplated in this framework and the Ministry has not participated in the development of the six joint programmes recently signed by the Federal Government of Somalia, the United Nations and donors in support of the New Deal commitments.[98] Key informants interviewed are concerned about the lack of formal arrangements for the participation of gender experts in PSG working groups, which is required to ensure that principles of gender mainstreaming and women's empowerment are applied to policy and programmatic decisions.

The UNDP strategy and how it developed

In preparing the country programme for 2011-2015, UNDP decided to adopt a twin-track strategy: (a) specific interventions in support of gender equality and women's empowerment; and (b) mainstreaming gender equality and women's empowerment in all other outcome areas where efforts were made to identify specific gender-sensitive outputs and indicators. UNDP Somalia also chose to adopt a specific outcome for gender equality and women's empowerment to address special interventions for creating fundamental structural changes in institutions, policies and legislation. The programme has four outputs as identified in the CPD which are presented in table 6 together with seven key intervention areas.[99]

The programme identified distinct needs and responses required for the Federal Government, Puntland and Somaliland. There were priorities cutting across the regions such as development of gender policies for the Federal Government and Puntland and implementation of the same in Somaliland; advocacy for including 30 per cent

Table 6. CPD outputs/sub-outcomes	
CPD original outputs (used interchangeably as sub-outcomes)	**Key intervention areas from the CPD**
Output 1. Gender equality and the empowerment of women implemented through advocacy initiatives in partnership with civil society and public institutions.	• Leadership, technical skills and advocacy capacity of women enhanced (incl. public speaking, facilitation, leadership and organizational management) to promote gender equality. • Targeted advocacy campaigns developed and dialogue spaces created on women's rights and role in society. • Capacities of men, particularly youth, traditional and religious leaders enhanced to advocate for women rights and gender equality
Output 2. Women's participation in peacebuilding, representation, civil service and public life increased at all levels.	• Organizational capacity of women's groups and networks strengthened to advocate for gender equality, including across zones.
Output 3. Women are empowered in social and economic development.	• Women's social and economic rights are legally recognized and protected.
Output 4. Women supported by appropriately designed, implemented and enforced legal and policy frameworks in line with the Convention on the Elimination of all Forms of Discrimination against Women, the Maputo Protocol and Security Council resolutions 1325 (2000), 1888 (2009), 1889 (2009) and 1820 (2008).	• Existing gender policies and legislation reviewed to identify gaps and improve government implementation. • Gender-based violence, including female genital mutilation, reduced through preventative measures

98   The six joint programmes totaling $120 million and commitments of $106 million were signed on 17 June 2015.

99   During the formulation of the programme for gender equality and women's empowerment, the four outputs have been elevated to sub-outcomes and used interchangeably. This was because the CPD programme outputs for gender equality and women's empowerment were formulated at a high level and almost impossible to achieve.

affirmative action representation in the constitutions, legislative assembly and district councils; and elimination of sexual and other forms of gender-based violence and FGM/C.

It was expected that UNDP interventions would lead to Somali women and men attaining greater gender equality and being empowered through: (a) changes in legal and policy frameworks; (b) institutions delivering as their mandates women and men who are empowered, demanding and accessing their rights; and (c) increased representation and participation of women and access of women to justice and legal protection. For these changes to happen, the programme anticipated the drivers of change to be women's organizations, government, religious leaders, traditional leaders, political parties and communities to change attitudes and behaviour on various aspects of gender equality and women's empowerment.

UNDP Somalia adopted gender mainstreaming in all programmes and projects as a strategy to ensure that the concerns and experiences of Somali women as well as men are an integral dimension of the design, implementation, monitoring and evaluation of the country programme; that gender disparities and/or discrimination do not continue or worsen in terms of opportunities, capabilities, empowerment and security. The incorporation of gender empowerment outputs and indicators under the different outcomes of the country programme ensured that gender issues are meaningfully addressed and mainstreamed across the outcomes. The original idea in the CPD was that interventions would go beyond being simply gender-sensitive and gender-responsive to be gender-transformative.[100]

Taking into account the strategic elements set out in table 6 and the evolution of the gender interventions over time, the ADR team categorized the contributions of development results for gender equality and women's empowerment in six areas:

a) contributing to political participation, leadership and decision-making;

b) contributions to justice and accessing legal protection;

c) prevention of sexual and gender-based violence and FGM/C;

d) advocacy for and public awareness of women's human rights;

e) contributions to policy and legal frameworks and awareness of international policy instruments for gender equality and women's empowerment;

f) women's economic empowerment.

Components at the output level

UNDP aimed to **contribute to decision-making** through more equal representation and participation of women as decision makers and enhancement of the quality of women's participation. UNDP support was aimed at capacity-building of female members of parliament (MPs) to understand the legislative process and spearhead gender advocacy.[101] At the federal level, women MPs benefited from practical and South-South cooperation through training by former Kenyan MPs.[102] Women's groups and individuals have gained knowledge and skills in Somaliland. Through gender mainstreaming in the joint programme on local governance, women's performance in political campaigning and public speaking was substantially enhanced.[103] In Puntland, the UNDP mainstreaming approach undertaken with the Ministry of Women and Family Social Affairs

---

100   UNDP country programme document (2011-2015).

101   Gender equality strategy 2013.

102   All MPs, including women MPs, benefited from the training.

103   Consequently, 172 women competed for 368 contested seats in local governments. Although women won only 10 seats, it is an improvement from two council seats won by women in 2002. Source: evaluation of joint programme on local governance and comments from key informants interviewed.

used a strategy that contributed to greater engagement of women candidates, 500 of whom were identified in 37 districts and 150 of whom were prioritized for party nominations.

Through **contributions to justice and accessing legal protection,** UNDP aimed first to empower Somali women to participate in the provisional constitutional development, which led to some minimal gains in gender-sensitive enforcement mechanisms of the Provisional Constitution.[104] Despite advocacy for a 30 per cent quota of women in all decision-making bodies, this was not integrated into the Provisional Constitution. Women have improved access to the legal system: UNDP supported 4,729 women with legal aid by formal courts, lawyers and paralegals; 542 women were assisted by mobile courts; and 326 survivors of sexual and gender-based violence received assistance through the sexual assault referral centre.[105] In Somaliland, 32 women who completed UNDP-supported graduate internship programmes were appointed chief registrars, prosecutors and government advisers. The Attorney General's Office established new Women and Children Units in Borama and Buroa.[106] In Puntland, UNDP supported the recruitment and training of female lawyers through scholarships and internships. A total of 42 female students attended the Puntland State University Faculty of Law. Graduates established the first Puntland Women Lawyers Association.

Efforts to **prevent sexual and gender-based violence** were aimed at strengthening the civilian police force in Somaliland, including training of 816 female police officers deployed to ensure a multisectoral response to such violence. Sensitization training was also held for senior police officers in Somaliland.[107] The targeted approach of UNDP to a women's network in Somaliland led to greater awareness and enhanced knowledge of NGOs, service providers and other stakeholders, including development of a judicial monitoring tool to collect, monitor, follow up and evaluate case proceedings. In collaboration with the Ministry of Labor and Social Affairs and the Ministry of Youth and Sports, UNDP raised awareness of 30,000-40,000 youth attending the Somaliland National Sports Tournament about sexual and gender-based violence, and more specifically rape, by using behavioural change communication materials in the stadium.[108] In Puntland, a gender-based violence criminal investigation officer was appointed and handled these types of crimes, although the ADR could not establish the case load and number of cases successfully concluded.

Advocacy and public awareness on women's human rights have aimed to promote women's participation in public life in the southern and central regions. Fifty selected women's rights advocates from different sectors were trained on human rights, women in Islam, leadership and women's participation in politics. Interviews indicated that they are able to advocate for women's participation in leadership and decision-making processes. Fifty women local leaders maintain regular meetings and information-sharing through the region.[109] In Somaliland, gender equality training provided to local government, traditional leaders and religious leaders has brought about attitudinal change: participants became advocates for women's rights. Through UNDP support to the Ministry of Women and Family Social Affairs, alternative livelihoods were provided to 60 FGM/C practitioners, helping to offset the loss of income from circumcising girls.[110] Sensitization workshops on FGM/C and sexual and gender-based violence

---

104 Gender equality strategy 2012.

105 ROAR, 2012, 2013.

106 ROAR 2013.

107 Gender equality strategy 2013 report.

108 ROAR, 2012, 2013.

109 Gender equality strategy 2013 report.

110 ROAR, 2013.

were conducted for some 5,176 participants, and 65,000 people benefited from radio campaigns and talk shows on gender equality. The gender equality and empowerment of women project provided specific capacity-building training for female district councillors and supported them in undertaking an advocacy campaign around the election activities, which had tangible results.

UNDP contributed to **policy frameworks and awareness of international policy instruments on gender equality and empowerment of women** through a targeted approach to influence policies and institutional structures in all three regions, but in some regions results still are not visible due to lack of government commitment. In Somaliland, an implementation plan for the Somaliland National Gender Policy was developed with UNDP support and an interministerial gender coordination mechanism established. In Puntland, advocacy for a gender policy continued to meet with stiff resistance from influential members of the cabinet with extreme religious views.[111] At the federal level, UNDP was able to sustain the support for a national gender policy, resulting in a road map for consultations and redrafting of the draft gender policy developed in 2013 by AMISOM. Sixty-two participants (17 men and 45 women) from the gender ministries and women activists were trained on international gender policy frameworks.

UNDP work for **women's economic empowerment** provided 60 tertiary scholarships to young women from disadvantaged backgrounds in Somaliland and Puntland. Over 900 women were trained with employable skills and provided with microgrants and start-up kits in Puntland. In Somaliland, 120 people living with HIV (65 per cent women) were trained and set up micro-enterprises with grants. In Puntland, UNDP provided material support to establish the Puntland Women's Multipurpose Centre (pending completion). UNDP interventions led to microcapital grants for seven CSOs across the Somali regions that conducted advocacy and awareness-raising on issues ranging from sexual and gender-based violence to livelihoods, gender justice, FGM/C and women's political participation.

FINDING: UNDP has contributed to building the foundation for greater gender equality and women's empowerment in Somalia but the limited size and scope of these initiatives limit their perceived relevance as being severely inadequate given the enormity of the issue.

In terms of contributing to decision-making, UNDP support is promoting more equal participation of men with women as decision makers and enhancing the quality of women's participation. However, improvements need to be made to reach a minimum of 30 per cent female participation in political forums. It should also be noted that that the results are not yet at the higher level of outcome; concrete change will emerge when MPs positively influence legislative processes; use a gender analysis to influence the forthcoming review of the Constitution; pass gender-sensitive legislation or gender policies; or when the Convention on the Elimination of all Forms of Discrimination against Women is ratified.

UNDP support has contributed to the protection of rights and legal systems benefiting men and women; UNDP is progressively mainstreaming gender in access to justice, leading to greater gender responsiveness on the part of the judicial, security and legal sectors, through capacity-building and increased representation of women in decision-making. Key informants interviewed commended the achievement of UNDP in the legal access and scholarship programme.[112] They also noted that while there has been marked progress in women's access to legal rights, more improvements are needed as

---

111 Government officials indicate that the main obstacle for passing the policy is the use of the term "gender equality" in the draft. USAID, Gender Assessment Report, 2014.

112 ROAR, 2012, 2013.

traditional institutions or clans continue to settle many cases concerning sexual violence and compensation for murder within a clan, with few benefits in favour of women and girls.

Through the combination of a targeted approach and mainstreaming, UNDP support is making small but significant steps in reducing sexual and gender-based violence. While this was a good approach, it was not accompanied by monitoring mechanisms and follow-up to ensure that women police officers were delivering gender-responsive policing. At the same time, information on the change that occurred after the trainings was not documented.

UNDP support has contributed to greater advocacy, awareness-raising and recognition by the public (women and men) and decision makers of the human rights of women. UNDP support is contributing to the formulation of national/regional policy frameworks and awareness of international policy instruments for gender equality and women's empowerment.

In Puntland, a gender mainstreaming approach in poverty reduction efforts led to improvements in women's skills and access to grants. In Puntland, over 900 women were trained in employable skills and provided with microgrants and start-up kits. In Somaliland, 120 people living with HIV were trained and set up micro-enterprises; 65 per cent of the targeted beneficiaries were women, who received training and grants to help them launch their micro-enterprises. However, key informants interviewed in both Puntland and Somaliland indicated that microgrants were of a short-term nature (six months or less) and UNDP hardly followed up on the change that occurred after the grants were awarded.

A number of factors can be identified to explain the performance described above. The first is the partnerships developed by UNDP, which worked with relevant stakeholders based on their mandate to bring about change on gender equality. Ministries of women or social affairs were relevant in playing a strategic role in implementing policies, coordination and evaluating progress in the advancement of women. NGOs and women's organizations were relevant in fostering peace, mobilizing and advocating for women's political participation, promoting awareness of gender equality, improving women's livelihoods and addressing harmful traditional practices such as FGM/C at local levels. Working with religious leaders and traditional leaders was relevant for effecting change in behaviour towards discriminatory practices.

Second, as noted earlier in this section, UNDP has made significant efforts to include gender concerns in its planning and has developed institutional and individual capacities of country office staff. While such planning processes are important, they are the means to achieve gender equality results rather than results in and of themselves. In the last two years, 68 programming staff received training on gender mainstreaming and the first training for operations staff took place in June 2014. UNDP Somalia applied the gender marker[113] as an effective tool for gender mainstreaming at formulation stage but it only indicates expenditure allocations, with no monitoring mechanism to assess whether those expenditures or budgeted activities translated into concrete results (table 7). The gender marker shows concentration of expenditures in GEN1 with the bulk contribution by outcome two projects. As expected, the programme's outcome 4 on gender has the largest share of GEN3 ratings, which makes up less than 1 per cent of total expenditure (the overall budget expenditure for GEN3 is 5.8 per cent). Outcome 1 falls mainly in GEN0, indicating low allocation of funding for gender equality.

---

113 Scores range on a scale between GEN0 (not expected to contribute 'noticeably' to gender equality outcomes) and GEN3 (gender equality as a principal objective of the output).

Table 7. UNDP Somalia office, progress in gender mainstreaming by gender marker rating, 2013								
Gender Marker Rating	**Outcome 1**		**Outcome 2**		**Outcome 3**		**Outcome 4**	
	Total no. of projects	**Total expenditure ($)**	**Total no. of projects**	**Total expenditure ($)**	**Total no. of projects**	**Total expenditure ($)**	**Total no. of projects**	**Total expenditure ($)**
GEN 0	0	0	3	1,836,210 (5%)	1	281,501 (0.7%)	0	
GEN 1	6	3,801,082 (10%)	15	17,845,740 (48%)	12	6,191,725 (17%)	0	
GEN 2	1	1,632,011 (4%)	3	4,249,824 (11%)	0	0	0	
GEN 3	0	0	0	0	0	0	2	1,433,034 (4%)

Source: ROAR 2011, 2012, 2013.

The publication, 'Gender mainstreaming made easy; a handbook for programme staff' is excellent but results can only be documented from those who have successfully used the handbook. It is noted that the original tool was applicable only for programming staff and not for operations staff. The 2014 gender training led to the development of a resource booklet for all programme and operations staff to fill this gap. Training on gender issues was provided regularly but the participants' evidenced transfer of learning from a training event to practice is what constitutes a result. The assessment through the Gender Seal will produce maximum results only when all the benchmarks have been achieved and the rating for UNDP Somalia moves from High Silver to Gold.

The most notable factor affecting the performance of UNDP in this area concerns strengthening of the Gender Unit with skilled staff who provided guidance in gender mainstreaming across outcomes, programmes and projects. The Gender Unit provided support for gender mainstreaming in a coherent and systematic manner supported by the UNDP Somalia Gender Focal Team, headed by the Deputy Country Director for Programming and with representatives drawn from all units, programmes and projects.[114] The ADR team concurs with the findings of the Gender Equality Seal that the composition of the Somalia office gender focal team is comprehensive and meets standards.[115]

The ADR team was made aware that the efforts are being championed only by ministers of women's affairs and that other ministries (such as ministries of education and justice) are not fully engaged and thus do not understand that it is a gender policy (for women and men) and not a women-only policy. UNDP worked more with female parliamentarians and had limited success in leveraging the support of influential male actors/champions to support the women's agenda. The Somaliland parliament removed discussions on the quota for women in the parliament from its agenda at the start of 2013. The only female member of the Guurti (House of Elders) resigned at the start of the year as a result of lack of support in a chamber where 81 of the full quorum of 82 members are male. According to key informants interviewed, the female member inherited the seat upon her husband's death and has been replaced by her son. The huge imbalance in representation is evidenced by the name of the group 'Aqalka Odayaasha', which in a literal translation from Somali means 'House of Male Elders'. The ADR notes that other factors are difficult for UNDP to penetrate in the short term, given that it is working in an environ-

---

114   Gender equality reports 2012 and 2013 and ROAR, 2013.

115   UNDP Somalia, Gender Equality Seal Report, 2013.

ment of deeply clan-based culture which promotes strict male hierarchy and authority.

On Security Council resolutions 1325, 1820, 1880 and 1889, UNDP implemented activities in line with the resolutions, such as increasing the proportion of women in decision-making in governance institutions and supporting institutions that provide state security, promote women's participation in peacebuilding, prevent sexual and gender-based violence and implement systems that ensure that women and girls have access to justice and law enforcement institutions. However, the ADR noted that there is no conscious linking with the resolutions and activities have been conducted as on-off events with little visibility.

There seem to be inconsistent and weak links in the use of a results framework as a tool for planning and reporting. The ADR team finds inconsistency in indicators for outcomes from the CPD and ROAR, (ref. ROAR 2013). In a few cases, UNDP Somalia has formulated 'one-off targets' that are not cumulative over the subsequent years, making it difficult to assess transformative results over a four-year period, for example, to establish a centre in year 1 but with no linkage with any targets for years 2, 3 or 4. This lack of cumulative targeting has in most cases led to UNDP initiatives being small-scale and short-term. It also impacted negatively on the effectiveness of results, for example, the short-term provision of microgrants through an NGO in Somaliland and another in Puntland which came to an end but with no follow-up even though it is within the CPD period.

The UNDP Somalia interventions in training and awareness-raising were expected to increase knowledge and change attitudes. The country office's rationale is that: (a) gender inequality prevailing in Somalia is the result of a strong patriarchal system which is culturally rooted; and (b) these are negative attitudes and behaviours acquired through socialization processes which can be addressed only through training, advocacy and awareness-raising. However, it is possible to determine whether the changes in knowledge and attitudes translated into changes in practice over time only with baseline data before and after the training. The ADR team finds no monitoring mechanism at the outcome level, for example such as by reviewing police records and interviewing complainants on their experiences with the handling of their cases to determine what changed. Getting baseline data in Somalia remains a challenge but UNDP relies on results and reports of its previous interventions as a baseline.

Overview

In Somalia, the HIV and AIDS situation is geographically heterogeneous, with low levels throughout the country except in Somaliland where it is concentrated with higher prevalence rates reported in locations of significant trade-driven mobility across all zones. The most recent rounds of antenatal care sentinel surveillance[116] found median HIV prevalence rates of 1.13 per cent in Somaliland, 0.41 per cent in Puntland and 0.25 per cent at the Federal level. The distribution of findings of HIV-positive testing among tuberculosis patients in health facilities, as well as those tested through voluntary counselling and testing, further corroborates the observation that the epidemic is more concentrated in Somaliland. Basic HIV and AIDS estimates are presented in table 8.

Table 8. HIV and AIDS estimates, 2013	
Number of people living with HIV	32,000
Adults aged 15 years and up living with HIV	27,000
Children aged 0-14 years living with HIV	5,400
Orphans due to AIDS aged 0-17 years	30,000
Adults aged 15-49 years prevalence rate	0.5
Women aged 15 years and up living with HIV	14,000
Deaths due to AIDS	2,500

Source: UNAIDS.

---

116   2011 in the case of the federal level and 2010 in the cases of Puntland and Somaliland.

All three Somali zones continue to work together closely in the HIV response and jointly prepared the HIV National Strategic Plan 2015-2019,[117] which includes three operational plans reflecting the regional differences. The plan was validated and endorsed in a meeting in Kampala, Uganda in April 2014 by representatives from all Somali zones, government (AIDS commissions and ministries of health), civil society, people living with HIV, key at-risk populations, the United Nations system and donors. The National Strategic Plan will guide the HIV response in Somalia for the coming years, including the development of the next proposal to the Global Fund to Fight AIDS, Tuberculosis and Malaria.

The Global Fund currently funds 95 per cent of all HIV work in Somalia. The current grant for Somalia of approximately $8 million per year ended in 2014. The grant covered all the costs of all antiretroviral treatment (ART) drugs and other HIV prevention, care and treatment work in Somalia. UNICEF is the principal recipient of the Global Fund grant in Somalia and a joint United Nations team on AIDS meets monthly. National AIDS commissions have been established in the Federal Government and in Puntland and Somaliland. In August 2014, Somalia submitted a new proposal to the Global Fund to support work in the period 2015-2017. However, the amount of the grant for Somalia is expected to be considerably less than the amount received for the last five years.

The UNDP strategy and how it developed

As a trusted development partner and co-sponsor of the Joint United Nations Programme on HIV/AIDS (UNAIDS), UNDP focuses primarily on building government capacities at all levels and working closely with civil society to support a coordinated and effective response to the HIV and AIDS epidemic.[118] HIV and AIDS was not highlighted in the CPD for 2011-2015 but is included in the results framework as an output: "[Millennium Development Goal] planning, programming and policy implementation capacities developed among partners for robust, participative analysis, including human rights, gender equality, HIV/AIDS".

The UNDP Somalia HIV and AIDS programme implements several stand-alone projects that are supported by the Global Fund. Over the period covered by this evaluation, UNDP has been the largest United Nations recipient of Global Fund resources in Somalia. In addition, the strategy has been to mainstream issues related to HIV and AIDS into the work of all other UNDP programmes. The main strategic priorities for country office are to:

a) strengthen the capacity of the national AIDS commissions;

b) strengthen district and community responses to HIV and AIDS in Somalia;

c) raise awareness through the media;

d) support networks of people living with HIV and AIDS.

Components at the output level

UNDP supports AIDS commissions in Somaliland, Puntland and the Federal Government to promote coherence and coordination at the regional and national levels, strengthen their relationships with other key partners (e.g., religious leaders and the media) and strengthen their capacities to better manage and coordinate the response to HIV in Somalia. UNDP provided technical support to the three commissions for the finalization and submission of the HIV concept note for the period 2015-2017 which was submitted to the Global Fund in 2014 after regional consultations. With UNDP support, the Somaliland AIDS Commission submitted an HIV proposal to the Global Fund that was approved for a grant of approximately $22 million for the period 2015-2017.

---

117   This replaced the previous HIV strategic framework that came to an end in 2013.

118   UNDP Strategic Plan, 2008-2011.

UNDP aims to **strengthen community responses** in order to generate social change in the fight against HIV and AIDS. It introduced the 'community conversations' initiative in 2011 to help communities to identify and discuss social norms and issues that make women particularly vulnerable to HIV infection. The conversations have helped to break the silence about HIV and gender issues. The project started in six HIV 'hotspot' districts in Somaliland and Puntland and later expanded to the Federal level. These gatherings often take place outside at a community centre or under a tree, where communities come together with the help of a facilitator to discuss how HIV is affecting their community. Since 2011, over 230,000 persons have benefited from the community conversations. The UNDP HIV unit also partners with NGOs that already work with the joint programme on local governance to roll out this project, with the intention that HIV and AID programming will be integrated into future district development plans.

The **HIV media project** worked with local radio stations in Somaliland, Puntland and at the Federal level to promote supportive attitudes towards HIV and highlight human rights and gender issues linked to HIV. UNDP supported training for local journalists to strengthen reporting on HIV and gender issues in which participants developed radio messages on HIV prevention, care and treatment. The project is helping to raise awareness of existing HIV services (e.g., voluntary counselling and testing, ART and medication to prevent mother-to-child transmission of HIV). In 2014, 1,464 messages on HIV issues were aired by seven radio stations.

UNDP **support to networks of people living with HIV and AIDS** promotes participation in planning, implementation and evaluation of AIDS responses. Greater involvement of people living with HIV and AIDS aims to help reduce stigma and discrimination.

Mainstreaming HIV and AIDS in the UNDP country programme included collaboration with the access to justice project to organize work-shops on 'Knowing your Rights' for people living with HIV, which reached approximately 500 people. As a result, UNDP legal aid services supported several people living with HIV to take up cases in court. The UNDP HIV Unit also worked with the poverty reduction and environment programme to start income-generating activities for people living with HIV. UNDP mainstreamed HIV awareness into its support to civilian police, including training of 40 members of the Special Protection Unit of the Somali Police Force and 150 policewomen on HIV and AIDS.

FINDING: UNDP has contributed to national efforts to fight HIV and AIDS, in particular to strategic planning, coordination and community response.

At the level of policy and coordination, where UNDP has focused on the national AIDS commissions, there is lack of understanding of the roles played by the commissions (strengthening and coordinating a multisectoral response) and the roles of the ministries of health (addressing all medical components of the HIV response), which has led to tensions between the two.

The community conversations appear to have been an effective approach in a very conservative country. According to the interviewees and internal project reports, the project resulted in positive changes in community attitudes towards HIV and AIDS, has driven an increase in voluntary counselling and testing activity and caused some women to cease working in the sex trade. As such, the project activities appear to have made significant contributions to the intended outcomes. However, no additional clear, evidence-based evaluation data were found to support this assumption. Evidence points to the implementing partner organizations having taken into consideration the cultural and religious sensitivities involved in discussing HIV and AIDS. They seem to have engaged religious and traditional leaders effectively and managed to impart some behavioural change.

The 'conversation' participants interviewed by the ADR data collection teams were very thankful to the implementing partner and to UNDP for the support they gave to people living with HIV. The participants claim to have established a strong sense of community and cooperation through the community forums, and the sessions have been a place for people to discuss other community problems aside from HIV/AIDS.

One of the implementing partners, Badbaado Team, received requests from all 16 villages of Bosaso to expand the programme due to its general popularity, and in 2014 the programme was extended to the village of Gibrile. The community contributed money for the construction of another community market, implementing recommendations and action points addressed during the community conversations. In addition, the mother and child health centre was constructed by the community with the support of the local council following the recommendations and consultations arising from the community conversations.

The findings indicate that gender is fully mainstreamed in the activities of the project. Women and men had the opportunity to participate in, contribute to and benefit from the project. The project has taken into consideration the different priorities and needs of the different beneficiaries. For example, there were special sessions for women and men, with other special sessions for youths and HIV/AIDS patients where necessary. As a result, the project promoted changes in male and female gender roles, attitudes and behaviour. In Somaliland, approximately 80 per cent of the participants were women, with fewer men attending the sessions partly due to the timing of the discussion sessions, which coincided with the afternoon 'chew'.

However, while UNDP-supported community conversations at Federal level, Somaliland and Puntland have yielded promising short-term results, there is very little evidence that UNDP has developed a convincing and replicable model for community-led initiatives through community conversations. The initiatives were generally small, short-term and relatively fragmented and their results have not been systematically monitored or documented. This last point is important and there needs to be more learning on the experiences if this approach is to be scaled up significantly. Inevitably, as the approach moves away from HIV and AIDS 'hotspots', its efficiency (in terms of its HIV and AIDS goals) will decline but there are opportunities to use the approach to introduce other issues, sensitive or not, that can contribute to further development and peacebuilding in Somalia. The community conversations approach needs to be part of the UNDP toolbox so it can be utilized when necessary. Funding could become an issue in the future due to the heavy dependency of UNDP on the Global Fund, but as the scope expands other sources can be mobilized.

4.2　THE RELEVANCE OF THE UNDP CONTRIBUTION

FINDING: UNDP interventions under all four outcome result areas were found to be largely relevant to the context, to national strategies and priorities and to local communities' needs, although in some cases more deliberate consultation with authorities and communities is required to further strengthen their relevance.

In the poverty reduction and environment programme, the vagueness of the strategic documents outcome (CPD, outcome paper, project document) contrasts with the very specific technical content of the programme in practice, i.e., as funded and implemented. The areas of work currently being pursued are generally quite reasonable and relevant. The problem with the programme as implemented is its very small size as compared to actual needs and to the new expectations created by the New Deal.

Support to the microfinance sector is mentioned prominently in the CPD and was pursued episodically by UNDP during the period under review, with engagement on the policy front (draft microfinance strategies and policies for Somaliland and Puntland) and a few hundred cases of project-administered credit at the grass-roots level, usually through local NGOs. Microfinance is not the simplest type of intervention to implement in a conflict context given the difficulty of collecting repayments, unless the Somali tribal channels are used. It is nevertheless relevant to continue support to the expansion of financial instruments and services by local banks and microfinance institutions.

The relevance of the 2012 national Human Development Report on youth stems from the absence of reliable data on socioeconomic development, and thus any additional well-researched document is welcome. The support to Somaliland and Puntland in drafting their development plans responds to the normal desire of the respective ministries of planning to structure their development goals and policies and is therefore very relevant.

Conceptually, it makes sense to regroup work on livelihoods and natural resources management, given that natural resources support the vast majority of Somali livelihoods such as pastoralism, agriculture or fisheries. The issue is once again, what difference can UNDP and its partners make on the ground in the environment sector? UNDP has access to Global Environment Facility resources and the machinery of international conventions, but how can it spend these resources most usefully, beyond helping to draft largely inapplicable national policies and action plans? The capacity to enforce state regulation would seem like a logical place to invest, rather than the drafting of additional plans.

The charcoal project provides an apt example of this problem. The United Nations joint programme for sustainable charcoal production and alternative livelihoods will focus on three components: (a) capacity-building and regional cooperation (by the United Nations Environment Programme (UNEP), involving advocating that countries in the region stop buying charcoal from Somalia); (b) development of alternative energy sources (the UNDP component); and creation of alternative livelihoods (by the Food and Agriculture Organization of the United Nations (FAO)). While each of these actions seems worth doing, it is unclear how they will make a significant difference to the trade of charcoal. The ban emanates from the Security Council and thus it has the highest international legitimacy, but it might not be as popular among local communities as it is in New York. Many people work in the charcoal trade[119] and many powerful people profit from it over and beyond al-Shabaab and, according to some, including members of the Kenyan military[120] present in the concerned areas (mainly around Kismayo).[121] The charcoal in question is of particularly high quality and in high demand in Gulf markets for the flavour it gives to meat. The problem is similar in essence to combating the production and/or trade of any illegal product, such as ivory or opium. The project document adopts a prudent livelihoods-based approach to the issue rather than an enforcement-based approach, and this is probably wise given the circumstances, but it is hard to see how anything less than a tough enforcement regime could curb such a profitable trade.

The solar energy project is perhaps the most obviously relevant project in the environment sector, with the supported hospitals in Garowe and Hargeisa reporting high satisfaction. The high cost of electricity in both capitals and the professionalism of the respective hospital staff who can maintain the solar panels in good working order (or ask the company for assistance) are

---

119   The men involved in clearing and burning are often in debt. See USAID Environmental Assessment.

120   Report of the Monitoring Group on Somalia and Eritrea pursuant to Security Council resolution 2060 (2012), S/2013/413, page 9, http://www.un.org/ga/search/view_doc.asp?symbol=S/2013/413

121   SWALIM Update Quarterly Newsletter, May - July 2013, Issue 2: SWALIM Locates Source of the Kismayo Charcoal Pile, at http://reliefweb.int/sites/reliefweb.int/files/resources/SWALIM%20Update%20Issue%202.pdf

two factors that make this simple project idea a successful proposition in the Somali context.

Under the governance outcome area, the access to justice work is fully aligned with the Six Pillar Strategy, which states: "Building a justice system in post-conflict Somalia is to make the people believe and trust the state and the statehood". The joint programme on local governance is equally aligned with the goal of investing in human capital "to ensure sustainable development in the future by guaranteeing access to basic services, fundamental rights and freedoms based on consensus and social peace." The support to constitution-making was fully aligned with the priorities of the Transitional Federal Government.

Perhaps because there is no single counterpart for broad capacity-building efforts, SIDP is an exception. The recent evaluation of SIDP noted that the biggest challenge for the project was that it was totally supply-driven. The evaluation found no strong evidence to show that the project had detailed consultations with the user line ministries before it was drafted and implemented. Moreover, Governments in Garowe, Hargeisa and Mogadishu told the evaluators that UNDP had brought "a list of things to support the Government", and that they (the Government) had no choice but to accept it. The report also notes that some of the plans and products developed by the consultants look more academic than practical and provide the example of the documents produced for the Office of the Auditor General, Puntland. Thus, while the project might make a lot of sense from an institutional development point of view given the context, its relevance is reduced by limited flexibility and engagement with primary stakeholders from the outset.

In the peace and security outcome area, the activities related to civilian police have been largely relevant and support the Federal Government's goal of a single Somali Police Force. Yet, while it can be argued that the community security work though the 'youth at risk' project is aligned to national priorities, these interventions are very small in relation to the overall issues that need to be addressed.

The UNDP gender programme was based on a very detailed situation analysis of the conflict and of the role of Somali women in peacebuilding; women in decision making; sexual and gender-based violence; and gender and social inequality. The programme was cognizant of the deeply rooted cultural male-dominated and clan-based system. A detailed analysis of the various (federal level, Puntland and Somaliland) gender perspectives informed the programme design and objectives.

As noted, UNDP Somalia made significant efforts to align its gender equality strategy to the corporate guidelines and strategies. The gender equality and empowerment of women programme was also aligned to the eight-point agenda for women's empowerment and eight-point agenda for girls and women in crisis[122] and Security Council resolutions 1325, 1820, 1888 and 1889.

Finally, UNDP support to the development of the basic infrastructure and policy frameworks for addressing HIV and AIDS, as well as raising awareness about the issue, have been relevant for the context and also for the UNDP mandate within the UNAIDS division of labour among United Nations agencies. Participants in interviews undertaken during field work in Puntland and Somaliland found the community conversations to be highly relevant in a context where opening dialogue, in a very conservative Muslim community on a subject regarded as a taboo, is key to changing people's attitudes

---

122   The eight points are: (a) strengthen women's security in crisis; (b) advance gender justice; expand women's citizenship; (c) participation and leadership; (d) build peace with and for women; (e) promote gender equality in disaster risk reduction; (f) ensure gender-responsive recovery; (g) transform government to deliver for women; and (h) develop capacities for social change.

     CHAPTER 4. THE UNDP CONTRIBUTION TO DEVELOPMENT RESULTS

towards HIV and AIDS. The selection of potential project sites was based on research on HIV and AIDS 'hotspots'. Based on this information, UNDP did an assessment to gauge the feasibility of implementing a pilot community capacity enhancement project in Berbera. The project was identified in consultation with the local community groups. With the presence of the local council of Berbera, the initiative was endorsed by different sectors of the community, albeit with some trepidation given the sensitive nature of the topic.

4.3 THE EFFICIENCY OF THE UNDP CONTRIBUTION

Efficiency is looked at two ways: programme efficiency; and management efficiency. The latter is addressed in chapter 5 in the section on management and operations together with issues related to strategic positioning.

FINDING: The successful mainstreaming by UNDP of cross-cutting programme components such as gender and HIV and AIDS into other interventions such the joint programme on local governance and access to justice enhances programme synergies and improves the potential for both effectiveness and efficiency. On the other hand, shortfalls are seen in annual programme expenditure targets due to funding and security constraints.

As noted above under the section of effectiveness, there have been many good examples where UNDP has mainstreamed programme components and promoted programme synergies. These include mainstreaming gender in access to justice, providing legal services to the poor and marginalized through access to justice, and including issues related to HIV and AIDS in the joint programme on local governance, so that the community conversations were included in district plans.

Regarding programme expenditure targets, with the exception of 2012 (83 per cent), the overall annual programme implementation rates were lower than the corporate threshold of 80 per cent (table 9). Factors that impacted implementation targets include slow funding flows to the Somali Compact and the security situation in some parts of the country.[123]

An expenditure analysis of sampled projects[124] shows that the largest proportion of programme

Table 9. Overall rate of programme execution, 2011-2014					
	2011	**2012**	**2013**	**2014**	**Total**
A. Programme budget*	73,346	83,719	67,133	69,538	293,736
B. Programme expenditure*	54,219	69,389	51163	52,147	226,918
C. Rate of (A/B)	74%	83%	76%	75%	77%

*Millions of US$
Source: Executive Snapshot (2015)

---

123 The United Nations was the target of the 2013 attack on the United Nations Common Compound in Mogadishu and the 2015 attack in Garowe, Puntland, both of which caused the death of United Nations staff and led to heightened security restrictions which impacted programme implementation.

124 Rule of law and security programme; Disarmament, demobilization and reintegration/armed violence reduction project in Somalia; Democratization and Constitution; Somali institutional and capacity development project; Local governance and decentralized service delivery support; Somali institutional development project; Civilian police project in Somalia; Access to justice in Somalia; Joint programme on local governance; Integrated watershed management; Poverty reduction and environment programme; Country office strategic gender mainstreaming; Country office gender support.

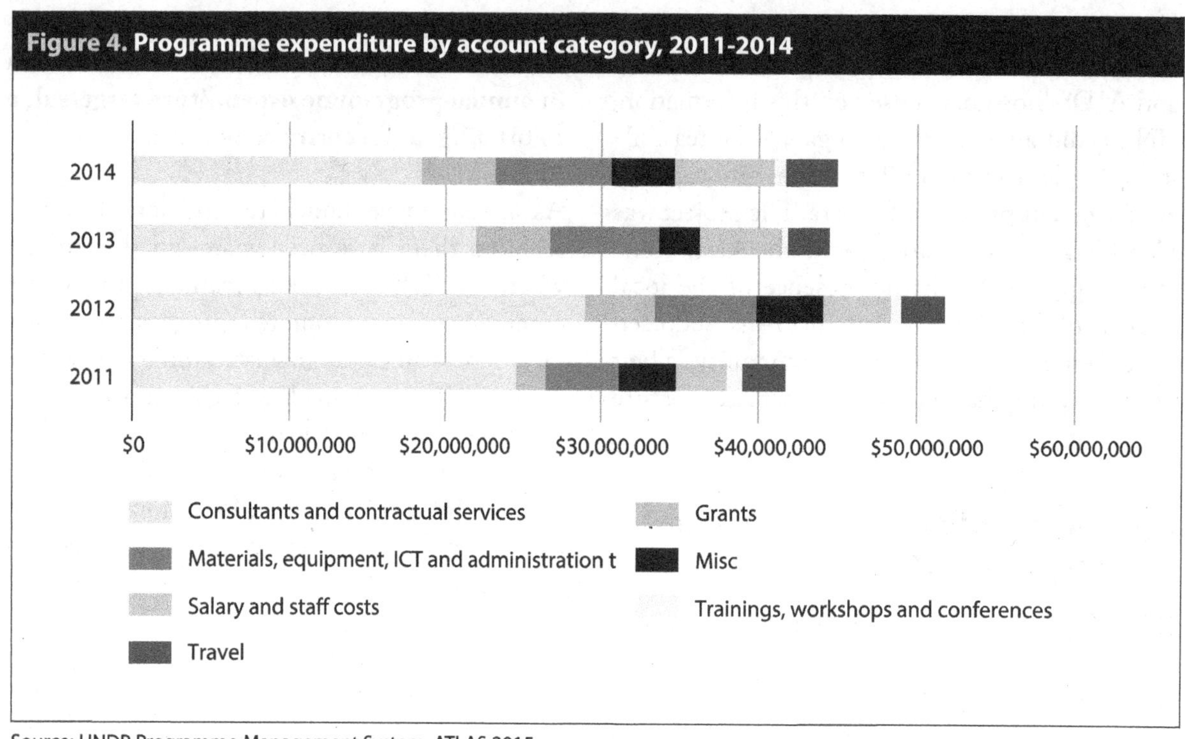

Source: UNDP Programme Management System, ATLAS 2015

expenditures was concentrated in activities in line with the UNDP role in providing advisory services and capacity development (figure 4).

4.4 THE SUSTAINABILITY OF THE UNDP CONTRIBUTION

FINDING: With the exception of some of the interventions implemented under outcome area 2, where national ownership is enhanced by capacity development and use of national institutions, the ADR found limited sustainability prospects for the projects and results to which UNDP contributed. Weak national capacities, fragmented capacity development interventions, availability of financial resources and insecurity in some areas of the country are the limiting factors.

While the sustainability of UNDP interventions will always depend on the availability of resources, the more important question concerns the sustainability of the results to which UNDP contributes. In the case of access to justice, although there is a limit to how long UNDP and its donor partners will be able to fund this work, the results are likely to be sustainable. This likelihood is enhanced by complementing training and scholarships with efforts to find employment for participants, even if initially only through internships. Equally, better use of national institutions such the University of Hargeisa to anchor the legal aid initiative enhance the likelihood of sustainability (notwithstanding the disagreement with the Ministry of Justice on its role in the legal aid system). Similarly, strong national ownership in the joint programme on local governance means that the results are likely to be sustainable and the Somaliland Government's use of the joint programme's approaches to expand the scheme is further evidence that the scheme has been institutionalized in that region.

In contrast, the internships funded through SIDP are less likely to be sustainable. The European Union evaluation report quotes the Deputy Minister of Planning and International Cooperation in Mogasishu as saying, "['Qualified Expatriate Somali Technical Support - Migration for

Development in Africa' project] recruits have come to Somalia as summer interns to earn some quick money and go back. There was no sustainable contribution from them." As already noted, the majority of SIDP deliverables were focused on capacity substitution, which severely reduces the likelihood of sustainability of results.

A number of beneficiaries from across all components who were interviewed by the ADR team noted that while UNDP support was extremely useful, the equipment provided was often old and needed replacing. This brings into question the sustainability of some of the results achieved through simple construction and procurement efforts (vehicles, uniforms, equipment, etc.) and the roadmap for government taking over such efforts as well as stipends.

In the poverty reduction and environment programme, security is of course a significant issue, notably in the south. In the north, a general lack of capacities, including financial capacity from governments, implies low prospects for sustainability in many of the reviewed cases. The solar panel project seems to be sustainable at least during the warranty period (five years) during which the hospitals can rely on the international company in case of breakdown.

Capacity development and vocational/youth training efforts are fragmented and almost systematically composed of short training sessions and workshops, which are not necessarily sustainable. From the point of view of sustainability – and this point is made very clear by the administrations and communities concerned – what is really required is a set of vocational training centres like the Burao Institute in Somaliland (see box 1) that would have better prospects of continuity, instead of a series of on-off trainings. The same applies to the training of civil servants, with the Civil Service Institute of Somaliland being pointed out as a model. More generally, there is a need to invest in institutions, e.g., use the universities and other training centres already in existence, rather than provide short-term training directly to youths, Sheikhs, district counsellors or ministry staff.

Similarly, the engagement on microfinance had been short-term prior to closure in 2013. In Garowe, some cash injection for women in previous years was apparently conceived as credit according to the implementing NGOs, but the project was short in duration and the credit not recovered. Microcredit is not something that can be done through projects lasting just 6 or 12 months. The lack of continuity means that the results are not adding up to something larger and are not cumulative, contrary to what could be the case with a more elaborate and sustained support to microfinance institutions.

Sustainability is an inherent issue with job creation programmes (cash for work, food for work), in that the future maintenance of the repaired infrastructure can never be the primary function of such projects, which are basically about creating short-term jobs. Poor maintenance capacity seems to be an issue affecting short-term work on feeder roads and other infrastructure. After all, the project rehabilitates public buildings and roads precisely *because* they have not been maintained properly in the first place by the concerned authorities.

The heavy reliance on NGOs also leads to low local ownership and sustainability. The only cases where the ADR team perceived a sense of strong local ownership, and therefore show good prospects for sustainability, was when the poverty reduction and environment interventions were implemented through local governments, e.g., within a partnership with the joint programme on local governance. In those cases (e.g., in Gardo or Eyl), the district council or mayor was in charge and capacitated to manage the infrastructures. More of these types of partnerships (and an expansion of the joint programme) would appear desirable from this point of view of building strong delivery and management partnerships at the local level.

UNDP support to civilian police also has limited prospects for sustainability, especially with respect to stipends. Sustainability also appears to be major concern about the community security projects. Further efforts are required to monitor the trainees, for example through tracer studies that track the participants once they have completed training. Data collected from Resource Centres for Peace suggest that while 'youth for change' staff have the local capacity to continue this work, they lack the financial resources to do so. It appears that no explicit sustainability plan is in place for the Resource Centres. After completion of the project, the beneficiaries transferred to the ILO skills training programme, which would build upon their social rehabilitation and help them to acquire more skills. However, the centres do not have the financial resources to continue with the recruitment of new students. It is also not clear whether UNDP will renew the project.

With regard to the gender equality and empowerment of women programme, the assessment of the gender-specific interventions is more positive. Appointing gender focal persons at ministries in the Federal Government of Somalia, Puntland and Somaliland, designing action plans and putting in place systems and structures for mainstreaming gender at ministries will assist in sustaining the progress made so far and institu-

tionalizing approaches to policy implementation. Some of the other approaches used by UNDP have potential for sustainability. However even in this situation, once change does occur in a community, it can be sustained only if village communities, in coordination with local government structures, enforce their decisions.

As to the sustainability of results of training to build individual capacities and competencies in gender mainstreaming, these are likely to be sustained. The commitment of UNDP programme staff and their partners to gender equality work, their motivation and interest in applying their new/increased knowledge and skills to their work and the opportunities for networking are all factors supporting the likelihood of participants' continued involvement and the sustainability of these activities.

The ADR team notes that capacity-building through training too often has been seen as a way to meet the 30 per cent quota in terms of female versus male beneficiaries.[125] While capacity-building is a positive step and shows a concrete output in the short term, it means that results are reported at output level disaggregated by the number and sex of people who received the training or attended a workshop. UNDP succeeded in providing individual skills training to programme staff and partners but there is room for improvement, going beyond numbers and addressing which capacities have changed at the level of an entity, organization, group or system (e.g., planning, laws, M&E, programme/project management, technical specialization). Representatives of key CSOs interviewed all wanted to see improved systems for their organizations.

UNDP Somalia was effective in strengthening structures for coordination of gender equality and empowerment of women in Somaliland and Puntland. In Somaliland, the programme facilitated the appointment of gender focal points and established an interministerial gender coordina-

---

125   This was also the finding of the 2010 ADR.

tion mechanism which provided a platform for the Government to discuss and make decisions on crucial gender-related matters such as whom to sponsor for scholarships.

On HIV and AIDS, while the community conversations were relevant, effective and efficient, their sustainability appears to be somewhat at risk. Field work in Puntland and Somaliland found that the implementing partner had requested further funding to continue the sessions, building on the project's achievements and with the aim of building the capacity of the local council to take over the sessions. In 2014, UNDP was successful in having some funds set aside to support HIV/AIDS work in five district plans. This linking of the community conversations with the joint programme on local governance is not only efficient but seems like an effective way to secure greater institutional sustainability, in turn leading to greater likelihood of the sustainability of results.

Chapter 5

MANAGEMENT, OPERATIONS AND THE STRATEGIC POSITIONING OF UNDP

This chapter focuses on two groups of factors that have affected the performance of UNDP in Somalia across all of the outcome areas of the ongoing country programme: (a) management and operations; and (b) strategic positioning. The former specifically includes issues related to management efficiency while strategic positioning is a factor that affects the performance of UNDP according to all criteria, but mostly effectiveness.

5.1 MANAGEMENT AND OPERATIONS

This section builds on the description of the management and operations in chapter 3 and tries to link the issues to UNDP performance. Four groups of factors have been identified: (a) the structure of the country office; (b) project implementation and supervision; (c) human resources; and (d) working as part of an integrated mission. Context plays a role in all these issues and for many of them it is also important to take into account the tragic events of June 2013.

STRUCTURE OF THE COUNTRY OFFICE. The complex structure of the Somalia country office, with offices across the five operational environments within which it works, creates extra challenges for effective management of the UNDP programme.

The sub-offices/area offices are the engines of delivery, particularly in the north where security conditions allow for smoother programme implementation, but they are located at the periphery of the UNDP structure in Somalia and have difficulty solving key administrative issues such as premise contract management. The

sub-office guidelines – branded as an example for UNDP worldwide at the time of development – are still the 'constitution' of UNDP in Somalia, but new practices have crept in. Even with a now very responsive management team positioned in Mogadishu, the Nairobi administrative support office is still required for many transactions and appears to be a much slower-paced place than Mogadishu or Garowe.

These issues have been further compounded by lack of clarity on reporting, responsibilities and supervision found during the main data collection in June 2014 but which have since been resolved. Two major issues noted by the 2014 audit of the country office,[126] in particular inconsistent organigrams between offices and inconsistent job descriptions between various managers, have since been addressed by UNDP Somalia management and deemed as closed by the Office of Audit and Investigation.

The country office has also since addressed other audit observations, including inadequate plans (business continuity plan, which includes a disaster recovery plan) to ensure the continuity of operations in the event of an unscheduled interruption of operations.

PROJECT IMPLEMENTATION AND SUPERVISION. Project implementation and supervision clearly face challenges in a conflict environment or even in the transitional context of Somaliland.

The 2014 audit identified a number of weaknesses at the office level: (a) erroneous recording

---

126   UNDP Office of Audit and Investigation, 'Audit of UNDP Country Office in Somalia', Report No. 1299, 20 June 2014.

of advances; (b) lack of capacity assessments for implementing partners; and (c) insufficient field verification visits. The audit report also identified a number of weaknesses at the project level including: (a) failure to sign project documents; and (b) weak oversight by project boards. The country office took immediate actions to address these issues.

Low delivery is also a direct consequence of the lack of robust capacity to screen (capacity assessment for prequalification) and monitor partners, which would assuage some of the concerns over corruption and the perceived need for many international staff. The UNDP corporate guidance for remote management and third-party monitoring emanates from the experience of the Somalia country office, and the experience was unfortunately discontinued in Somalia at the time of the move to Mogadishu. The recent move to place policy and planning advisers at area office level is also welcome, as is the institution of a third-party monitoring system in June 2015.

Related to the lack of capacity of implementing partners, UNDP in Somalia did not implement the harmonized approach to cash transfers (HACT) framework until September 2014. The HACT calls for a central (UNCT-wide) process of vetting and monitoring implementing partners. But even within UNDP, there was a need for greater centralization of files on implementing partners, since there seem to be cases where one UNDP programme discovers by chance that it works with the same implementing partner as another. Since September 2014, no new agreements have been signed without a micro-assessment. All new letters of agreement/microcredit grants incorporate prior capacity assessments and corresponding risk mitigation plans. Assurance activities (spot checks, audits and programme monitoring) are another important component of HACT, but the country office has yet to implement spot checks and audits even though programme monitoring is being undertaken.

Government and civil society implementing partners met by the ADR team expressed much frustration about delays, some lasting months, in approving letters of agreement and provision of funds. This is not always the fault of UNDP but nonetheless there seems to be a common view that processes through Nairobi take far too long. Other reasons for the delays in letters of agreement were the events of June 2013 and the subsequent shortage of senior management. Since then, the country office has revised the Local Project Appraisal Committee process to streamline it and reduce the time required for project approval. In 2014 the approval of annual workplans resulted from the need for revision to improve quality and they were only approved (internally) by the end of May. There was not sufficient communication to explain to partners why payments were delayed. Many of these issues are well known to management and while steps are being taken to address them, time is of the essence.

The issue of insufficient scale is linked with a slow delivery process, and with budgets and programme structures that appear quite top-heavy at the country level for a number of reasons. First, there are a limited number of technical staff who tend to be drawn into administrative and planning tasks, combined with an excessive reliance on international staff, which adds to costs but also to a generally low level of consideration for the Somali context in the earlier programme documents, including the CPD and the governance and rule of law and poverty reduction and environment project documents.

As is frequently the case in such fragile contexts, the multiplicity of offices in Mogadishu, Garowe, Hargeisa and Nairobi, coupled with difficult security conditions on the ground, results in significant costs for armoured cars, guards, rest and recuperation travel, etc. and can interrupt programme delivery.

Programme managers in Mogadishu should travel to sub-offices (Hargeisa, Garowe) more frequently but this also increases the cost and negatively affects efficiency. Moreover, their presence in Mogadishu means that their thoughts are more focused on Mogadishu, although the climate for long-term development is presently more conducive in the north.

Another factor is context. Doing business in Somalia requires a lot of care, which tends to slow down programme implementation. For instance, in Puntland where the level of corruption used to be quite high under the previous cabinet, UNDP had frozen cooperation with several government units due to a number of embezzlement cases.

The perception that UNDP is slow and delivers little may, however, be due to the fact that there were relatively new governments at federal level and in Puntland and Somaliland which were eager to show progress, albeit with limited capacities, and which may not be used to the pace of the United Nations. UNDP has been busy establishing contacts and understanding new priorities. The New Deal Compact is very process-oriented. It has generated much talk and many expectations, but received no new funding until mid-2015. This contributed to low efficiency for the first year of the Compact because the level of activity was not as high as envisaged, and because participating in programme support group meetings was actually taxing, and in the case of the poverty reduction and environment team, had no clear advantage for the programme. UNDP has been the lead actor for many UNCT initiatives in Somalia, particularly in the development and design of the joint programmes under the MPTF. By mid-2015, eight projects[127] had been approved by the MPTF with UNDP playing a lead role. Programmes with UNDP as a participating agency include:

a) PSG 1: support to the Federal State formation process (over $3 million); constitutional review and implementation support (over $4 million); support to the electoral process in the Federal Republic of Somalia (over $6 million); support to building inclusive institutions of Parliament in Somalia (over $11 million);

b) PSG 2 and PSG 3: joint rule of law programme (over $66 million);

c) PSG 4: joint programme on youth employment (over $8.9 million);

d) PSG 5: joint programme on local governance and decentralized service delivery in Somalia ($145 million);

e) Cross-cutting: joint programme on capacity-building (over $12 million).

HUMAN RESOURCES. Two issues can be identified in the area of human resources that may have affected the development performance of UNDP: (a) the degree of uncertainty that resulted from the relocation of the country office and the disruptive attack of June 2013; and (b) the gender equality dimension of human resources.

The full relocation of the country office from Nairobi to Mogadishu was planned in 2013. The relocation plan was initially phased over a 24-month period but later expedited to be completed in 12 months, by the end of 2013. After the attack, most international staff were displaced back to Nairobi or temporarily reposted to Hargeysa and Garowe, national staff in Mogadishu worked from home and, unsure about the future of the office, Nairobi-based staff received short-term contract extensions for nearly a year.

The new management arriving in late 2013 took measures to reduce this uncertainty among staff members and decided to extend the existence of the office in Nairobi for the foreseeable future. The current senior management clearly has a better understating and approach, and consequently an office retreat was perceived as very positive and inspiring.

---

127 Joint programme on local governance and support to building institutions of Parliament include budgets from previous years.

The second issue concerns the gender equality dimensions of human resources. A Gender Equality Seal assessment in 2013 rated the country office poorly at 2 out of a maximum of 9 points on its enabling environment for specific variables which included:

a) low performance in gender parity with fewer females than males at all levels;

b) no clear gender parity targets set and no actions for achieving them;

c) female staff account for less than half of the international positions;

d) gender disparity is more pronounced at the sub-office level.

The Gender Equality Seal process was conducted again in January 2015. Overall the office achieved a High Silver award and while the specific score for enabling environment factors has gone up (6 points out of 12), there is room for improvement. The Gender Seal team documented a range of issues addressed by the current management to promote gender equality. These include a greater proportion of women in the senior management team. In mid-2014 there was a single female at P4 level on the nine-person senior management team, compared to four women in May 2015.

Gender parity within UNDP at all levels remains a concern and key informants within UNDP and the United Nations system as well as donors are fully aware of the need to address the issue. The Somalia office shows an overall ratio of 2 males per 1 female (190/84). At P3 level and above, 74 per cent of staff are males compared to 26 per cent for females (see figure 5).

The ADR team was made aware of some factors that contributed to the low parity rate for

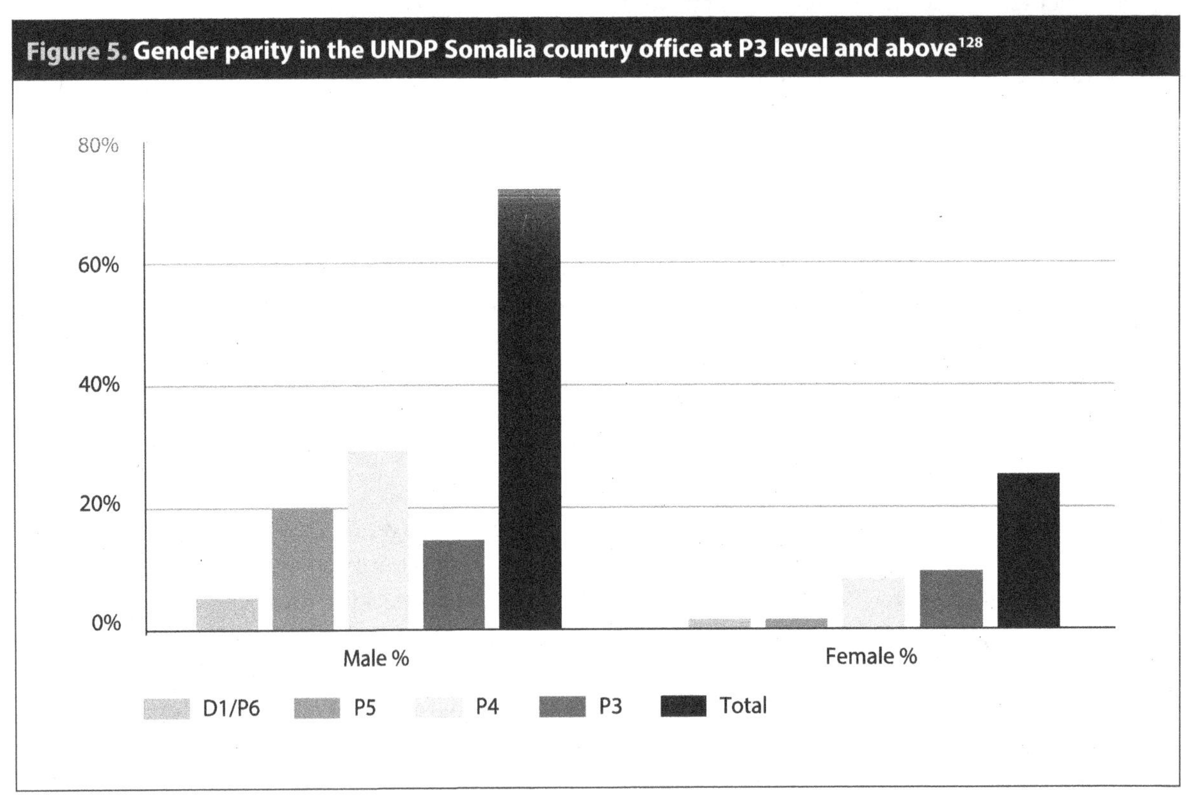

Figure 5. Gender parity in the UNDP Somalia country office at P3 level and above[128]

---

128   Note: This includes staff administered by UNDP for UNDP.

Table 10. Analysis of gender parity by applicants to posts in Somalia country office			
Level of Job	Number of posts	Female applicants %	Male applicants %
P2	1	= 31	= 69
P3	7	< 25	> 75
P4	3	< 20	> 80
P5	4	< 17	> 83
SC10	4	< 6	>94
SC9	10	< 23	> 77
SC7	1	= 25	= 75
GS6/SC6	5	< 15	> 75
SC5	1	= 5	= 95
GS5	1	58	42

Source: UNDP Somalia, Human Resources Unit, 2014

females; given the difficult context of Somalia, a limited number of female candidates apply for positions (on average 20 per cent of the applicants). A review of 39 applicants to posts in the Somalia country office over the last two years shows that fewer than 25 per cent of applicants for jobs in all Somali duty stations and at all levels were female, except for two posts in Nairobi (a human resources assistant and a project assistant, for which over 50 per cent of applicants were female) and one in Garowe (gender officer) (see table 10). In the case of international posts, the number of female applicants is relatively low; for example, a P5 post had only four (5 per cent) female applicants compared to 74 males (95 per cent). Surprisingly for a P5 post (trade economist) in Nairobi, only 8 per cent of applicants were female compared to 92 per cent male. Few Somali women are applying for jobs (levels SC10, SC9). Even for the gender officer post in Garowe, there were 36 female and 64 male applicants. The implications of these percentages is that reaching gender parity becomes a huge challenge when the pool of female candidates is small.

The country office gender equality strategy/action plan includes gender parity targets with specific actions, with progress reviewed at least twice a year by the senior management team. The office has started to circulate job announcements to women's networks.[129] The office also reports that national professional job announcements in Mogadishu have been re-advertised in an effort to attract women candidates. This is a reflection of the prioritization of and commitment by senior management to recruit more women.

WORKING AS PART OF AN INTEGRATED MISSION. While the ADR team had very little time to make a thorough assessment of the effectiveness of the integrated mission's arrangements and the role of UNDP in that mission (the mission structure was described in chapter 3 and is still relatively new), it is nonetheless possible to draw on a recent review of the global focal point system, which noted that UNSOM offers one of the clearest examples of the United Nations delivering integrated police, justice and corrections initiatives.

---

129   UNDP Gender Equality Seal Gold Office Matrix, Somalia Office Scores, January 2015.

5.2 THE STRATEGIC POSITIONING OF UNDP IN SOMALIA

Given the different work environments it faces in Somalia, UNDP has no single 'strategy position' for the country. In reality, its strategic positioning varies significantly across the three areas where it works, reflecting the very different contexts that have been described earlier. UNDP has made efforts to remain relevant to national development priorities through alignment with larger frameworks, most recently the New Deal. This approach, while pragmatic, has required UNDP to make several adjustments to its programme since it was designed in late 2009-early 2010, including most recently with the New Deal. This section will examine issues related to its strengths and partnerships with different groups of stakeholders.

COMPARATIVE STRENGTHS. The main comparative strength of UNDP lies in its long presence in the country, which is supposed to be reinforced by setting up offices in Mogadishu.

The proximity to some parts of the different governments (by no means universal) remains a strong advantage, together with the capacity to work with a variety of actors. UNDP played an important coordinating role during the development of the New Deal, followed up by strong support to the Aid Coordination Unit. Government officials, the United Nations system and donors acknowledged the continued lead coordination role of UNDP, for example during the development of the newly signed joint programmes. At the same time, the current situation in Mogadishu, while tenable, does not allow for much real presence in the south and central regions. Access is better in the northern regions but still limited. The traditional strength of UNDP in terms of helping Governments to plan their development, including through Millennium Development Goal planning, has been hampered in Somalia by the political discussion around the New Deal, a discussion in which UNDP and other United Nations development agencies seemed to play a limited role. The potential for UNDP to access large sources of financing will, however, depend on its ability to develop a credible delivery channel and technical means to reduce poverty or manage natural resources in Somalia. Through chairmanship of the United Nations Operations Management Team, UNDP contributes to UNCT operations, including management of facilities in Mogadishu and the regions, and cost sharing of the security budget.

Many staff members in the Federal Government of Somalia and authorities in Puntland were new to their positions at the time of the ADR mission. Government partners displayed a certain impatience with UNDP, which they generally consider too slow and too small. This is especially true at state level in the north, where the sentiment is that Mogadishu is getting most of the attention from donors and United Nations agencies discussing the New Deal, while in fact Somaliland's and Puntland's relative security and peace allow development to progress and should be rewarded by donors through 'peace dividends'.[130]

Local governments represent an opportunity, in particular because the joint programme on local governance is also supporting their capacities to plan and monitor local development. Although a number of NGOs did an excellent job, in the livelihoods sector the work with district councils, mayors and district peace committees (youth at risk) represents the best, most significant, effective and potentially sustainable elements of the evaluated work. In short, local governments can offer somewhat more stable delivery mechanisms than NGOs. They are of course not always honest and not without weaknesses, but NGOs have their improprieties too. More of these types of partnerships (and an expansion of the joint programme) would appear desirable from the point of view of building stronger delivery and management partnerships at the local level.

At the same time, government and civil society partners are often very frustrated with process. A serious problem is that expectations were not managed well in the past and programme managers seem to have been overly optimistic. They had a habit of presenting aspirations rather than realistic budgets but this issue is being addressed. This also affects the credibility of UNDP in the Government's eyes and this is becoming clear in Somaliland. In the recent past when not so many international organizations were helping Somaliland, the presence and long-term commitment of UNDP to Somaliland made it different from many other partners, e.g., international private sector implementing partners commissioned by donors. There is a risk, however, that all the goodwill that has been built up over the years could be thrown away through mismanaged expectations. Senior officials in Somaliland made it clear that they would prefer to work with the private sector than the United Nations.

DONOR PARTNERSHIPS AND RESOURCE MOBILIZATION. UNDP is operating in the context of limited resources and a changing resource mobilization environment. Its local presence in Mogadishu, Garowe and Hargeisa, costly as it is, allows it to play an intermediary role between donors and national authorities. This strategic posi-

---

130 Officials in Somaliland and Puntland evidently fear that the Federal Government will take the lion's share of the expected donor funding. Another perceived risk at state level is that instability in southern and central regions or other 'game spoilers' (e.g., inability to agree on how the money should be spent) could delay the funding forever until the ODA limelight shines on another country.

tion is common in conflict-affected countries, but in Somalia it is resented by both donors and government.

UNDP was perceived by donors neither as a strong intellectual leader nor as a strong, dependable operational channel for programme delivery. This perception is slowly changing and efforts by the new UNDP senior management to be more transparent and open have been acknowledged by some donors. The situation is now more open than it used to be; the World Bank is a new and assertive actor, and although it was not yet on the ground,[131] it is preferred notably in discussions relative to the New Deal. According to one government official, joint programmes involving the World Bank were immediately approved by donors whereas those of the United Nations were subject to negotiations. More private firms are also getting large implementation contracts from donors.

Compared to the governance and rule of law programme, the poverty reduction and environment programme has had modest success in mobilizing resources, despite UNDP being ideally positioned to raise funds in Somalia. This evaluation concludes that the dearth of credible, tested and scalable implementation strategies in UNDP programme documentation, as well as the absence of a third-party monitoring capacity through most of the country programme period, largely explain why the poverty reduction and

environment programme is currently attracting the donor resources it requires to scale up significantly. A robust system of implementing partner capacity assessment, monitoring and strengthening launched by the country office will be very useful in a country where UNDP can act only through other partners. The current 'systems' for monitoring and enforcing fiduciary rules are very ad hoc and depend on programme managers. This amounts to a central weakness in the current strategic positioning, based on the relatively strong field presence and delivery capacity of UNDP. The offices and embassies of donor representatives in Nairobi are staffed with people experienced in conflict countries and who often have counter-insurgency profiles. From what the evaluation can tell, they can generally draw on a certain degree of operational astuteness and are seeking credible, documented (hence evaluated) modus operandi in a difficult environment, which is significantly more than some UNDP project documents can offer.

In Somaliland, for example, donors have started to develop alternative aid delivery mechanisms such as the Somaliland Development Fund (see box 3) which is funded by the United Kingdom Department for International Development (DFID), the Danish International Development Agency (DANIDA), Norway and the Netherlands. The current contribution by the four donor countries currently stands at $60 million.

Box 3. The Somaliland Development Fund

The Somaliland Development Fund provides a single vehicle through which donors can support Somaliland's development goals. The Fund supports the Government of Somaliland, filling a critical gap by funding projects that are fully aligned to the National Development Plan, 2012-2016 while at the same time recognizing the role of the Government in the delivery of basic services.

The Somali Development Fund will also support the Government's communication of results to build accountability and transparency. Furthermore, the Fund is designed to strengthen the state-citizenship relationship and enhance accountability and domestic revenue generation. This in turn should lead to more stability and prosperity in Somaliland.

Source: http://www.somalilanddevelopmentfund.org/about

---

131 As of mid-2015.

All partners appear to be unhappy about one issue: the inability to show results. UNDP is undertaking many activities but the results (changes to people's lives or to institutions) are often unclear. This is an issue that goes beyond third-party monitoring of implementation and outputs (fiscal accountability) to concern the actual outcomes of the work, i.e., to answer the questions, what works, why has it worked, for whom did it work and in what contexts would it work again? It means doing baseline surveys and perhaps visiting the project months or years after it has been completed. It means treating evaluation not as an afterthought by which time it is too late but as a tool for learning, accountability and, where appropriate, resource mobilization. This is especially important in 'pilot' or other limited interventions that are expected to be replicated once resources are available or to feed into policy development processes. Of course, the nature of UNDP interventions means that they often address issues that are inherently long-term in nature and it is often difficult to see results in a few years (e.g., you can easily train and equip police but it can take years for attitudes to change). The context in which UNDP is working has also been one of continuous flux with repeated turnover of staff.

Nonetheless, donors rightly demand better information from their partners. For example, the Somalia Stability Fund is a multi-donor[132] fund designed to support peace and stability in Somalia, predominately through Somali partners in government, NGOs and the private sector. The Fund appointed the Somali-owned and managed Heritage Institute of Policy Studies to set up a research, evaluation and learning unit that will study a sample of funded projects and simultaneously contribute to an assessment of the entire portfolio. Researchers will be able to access tools allowing them to explore a variety of data, sourced through multiple and diverse methods. Donors expect nothing less from UNDP.

UNDP AND THE UNCT. Although coordination and establishment of partnerships with other United Nations agencies have met with variable results in the first half of the country programme period, between 2014 and 2015 UNDP played a central role in convening United Nations agencies around six new joint programmes and led the United Nations system in negotiations with donors.

UNDP works with the UNCT and various sector working groups, for example on gender and sexual and gender-based violence. Within the governance and rule of law programme, UNDP has successfully built partnerships with the joint programme on local governance (with ILO, UNCDF, UN-Habitat and UNICEF), the 'youth for change' project (ILO and UNICEF) and the joint rule of law programme. In the livelihoods and environment sector, UNDP appears somewhat isolated, with only the joint programme on youth employment (with FAO, ILO and UN-Habitat) and three small environment projects with UNEP.

In 2012, three United Nations agencies (FAO, UNICEF and the World Food Programme (WFP)) approved the joint resilience strategy aimed at promoting community resilience in Somalia. The strategy involves strengthening the productive sectors (FAO), improving basic social services (UNICEF) and establishing safety nets (WFP). The strategy also recognizes the need for an enabling policy and regulatory framework for effective service delivery and good local governance, but the agencies did not reach out to involve UNDP. The issue was discussed in the following terms in a recent evaluation of the FAO Somalia country programme:

> *FAO Somalia has chosen to focus its resilience strategy at the household and community level, but a wider systems–approach would appear to be more appropriate to the concept. Indeed, this has triggered lively discussions, especially in Nairobi,*

---

132   United Kingdom, Sweden, Denmark, Netherlands, European Union, Norway and United Arab Emirates.

about the extent to which governance issues should be included in the three-agency strategy, and therefore why other [United Nations] agencies such as UNDP are not key players in the strategy.[133]

In short, a good argument can be made that UNDP should have been involved in the strategy, but it wasn't. This apparent exclusion (confirmed by UNDP) may be little more than a banal clash of egos, but whatever the case, it provides an unfortunate illustration of the lack of strong bonds between UNDP and other United Nations agencies that was prevalent during the first three years of the country programme period.

---

133   FAO Office of Evaluation, 'Evaluation of FAO's Cooperation in Somalia, 2007 to 2012', May 2013 (para. 226).

Chapter 6

CONCLUSIONS AND RECOMMENDATIONS

The Somalia ADR aims to provide both an evaluation of the ongoing and planned activities of UNDP during the period examined, and a set of recommendations for improving the UNDP contribution to Somalia's efforts to achieve its developments goals. The conclusions and recommendations provided in this ADR are based on the findings presented in chapters 4 and 5 and are expected to contribute to better positioning of UNDP during the next programme cycle. The conclusions should be seen within the complex programming context and the challenges UNDP faces in contributing to development results in Somalia. The recommendations highlight only the most critical areas in which UNDP could enhance and consolidate its contribution, bearing in mind its mandate and comparative strengths.

6.1 CONCLUSIONS

Conclusion 1. The United Nations as a whole and UNDP in Somalia come under a lot of criticism based largely on the failures of the peacekeeping missions of the 1990s but also based on more recent performance, including the work of UNDP work in the governance sector (deemed by many internal and external observers to be political, externally driven and too ambitious).[134] This backdrop, combined with Somalia's peculiarly challenging programming environment, makes it even more important to qualify the performance of UNDP in the given context.

The ADR finds that UNDP made important contributions to Somalia's development efforts.

Given the depth and breadth of development needs and a limited enabling policy environment in Somalia, UNDP made important contributions to intended outcome result areas over the past four years. Examples of effective support by UNDP for Somalia's State-building efforts include support to the development of the Provisional Constitution and Parliament. For the first time in over two decades, Somalia has a Constitution which is in use. Despite critiques of the document itself, which underscores the shortfalls of the drafting process, the Constitution is increasingly used as a frame of reference by the Government and public. Similarly the Parliament, while not free of corruption allegations,[135] is also functional and resolving executive disputes through legislative action.[136] UNDP made its contribution in an extremely difficult and complex context that reflects both a challenging political environment and serious security issues. UNDP has had to be flexible in its programming to adjust to the changing context and also to the major changes in the international cooperation architecture introduced in the Somali Compact.

While generally effective, UNDP faced challenges to efficient implementation due to the high costs of maintaining adequate security for its operations. The need to maintain area offices

---

134   See for example, Menkhaus, K, 'A Country in Peril, a Policy Nightmare', ENOUGH Strategy Paper, September 2008; Hashi, A, 'Somalia's Vision 2016: Reality Check and the Road Ahead', The Heritage Institute for Policy Studies, May 2015; Mosley, J, 'Somalia's Federal Future: Layered Agendas, Risks and Opportunities', Chatham House, Royal Institute for International Affairs, September 2015.

135   See United Nations Monitoring Group on Somalia and Eritrea, Somalia Report dated October 2015.

136   For example, during recent episodes of political infighting, the Government did not come to a standstill as might have happened in the past. The disputes between the President and the two previous Prime Ministers were referred to Parliament where a vote of confidence ousted both Prime Ministers with significantly less delay than in the past.

and work in five different environments also effects efficiency in terms of getting value for money. Most importantly, UNDP rebounded from the significant disruption following the tragic events of June 2013 which inevitably disrupted parts of the programme. It is difficult to assess whether the decision to reopen the UNDP country office in the United Nations Common County Compound in early 2013 was the correct one. The political, practical and symbolic imperatives combined with pressure from many sides made the move inevitable but with the benefit of hindsight, UNDP could have been more cautious and realistic in phasing the transition. Even now UNDP is at greater risk than it would be in the compound at Mogadishu International Airport because it recognizes the need to be close to national partners, to have regular meetings which may not always be possible or convenient at the airport compound. This trade-off between security and effectiveness is difficult to manage, especially in such a fluid security environment but nonetheless demonstrates the continued commitment of UNDP to supporting the Government of Somalia.

Following the attack on its staff, the management of UNDP Somalia dedicated much time in 2014 and the first half of 2015 to addressing the operational issues that affect the effectiveness and efficiency of UNDP interventions, including those identified by the recent UNDP audit. While there is still some way to go in overcoming negative perceptions of UNDP among donors and United Nations agencies,[137] there is recognition of these efforts. New funding is available for six new joint programmes. UNDP is communicating more with donors and other United Nations agencies, as demonstrated by its lead role in negotiating with donors on behalf of participating agencies during the development of the six joint programmes signed in June 2015. Internally, the country office's management is to be commended

for assuming an adaptive approach in the human resources relocation strategy following the attack in 2013. Management's commitment to advancing gender equality, as demonstrated by achieving in January 2015 the High Silver award under the corporate Gender Equality Seal shortly after receiving the Bronze award, is also notable.

Conclusion 2. While the programme and its components generally have been relevant to Somalia's development needs, there has been much greater emphasis on contributing to development, peace and security through addressing governance issues compared to making a contribution through strengthening livelihoods. If UNDP Somalia is to make a meaningful contribution to the UNDP corporate vision[138] of eradicating extreme poverty and significantly reducing inequality and exclusion in Somalia, then greater investment is required to strengthen livelihoods.

The same issue was noted in the previous ADR, which recommended that UNDP "should strike an appropriate balance between interventions in support of building capacity of government institutions and initiatives to help address, in the short and medium term, the chronic development needs of the vulnerable groups of population, with a view to achieving progress towards [Millennium Development Goals], including on pressing issues related to environment". While efforts were indeed made to address the issue in the design of the next country programme, expenditures to contribute to the relevant country programme outcome (outcome 3) have amounted to less than 10 per cent of total expenditures over the period 2011-2014, as opposed to the expectation of closer to 40 per cent.[139] This has led to programme fragmentation with either small interventions that are a 'drop in the ocean' or the inability to maximize the contribution through achieving a critical mass of interventions in one place.

---

137   The ADR mission of June 2015 travelled to Nairobi and met with a limited number of donors, United Nations staff and government officials, in addition to UNDP staff.

138   UNDP Strategic Plan, 2014-2017.

139   As contained in the CPD 2011-2015.

   CHAPTER 6. CONCLUSIONS AND RECOMMENDATIONS

The UNDP Somalia programme is not unique in this respect and a similar situation was found in the ADRs of other fragile States including Afghanistan and the Democratic Republic of Congo. Inevitably, most UNDP programme resources must come from the donor community and other international partners. But with donors recognizing that the UNDP niche in Somalia is in the areas of justice, policing, political governance, electoral processes and local governance, areas that donors want to fund, the question arises as to how UNDP can persuade donors that it also has comparative strengths in the areas of livelihoods and poverty reduction.

One positive unintended outcome of this financial shortfall is that the country office was able to enhance programme synergies through mainstreaming and applying cross-cutting approaches between the different programme components. For example, UNDP governance programmes (outcomes 1 and 2), while not directly focused on income generation, do ensure that the poor and excluded benefit from mainstream development processes. Access to justice is about ensuring that the poor and marginalized have access to legal services; work on HIV and AIDS is supporting an excluded group; and the joint programme on local governance was intended to emphasize strongly equity and participation of marginalized groups. Nonetheless, while promoting democratic governance may be an essential part of the development and peacebuilding processes,[140] UNDP still needs to find the appropriate balance.

Conclusion 3. UNDP faces the challenge of remaining relevant across three very different operating environments while working through a single country programme. There is a trade-off between the practical reality of adapting to different environments and the need for programme coherence. Yet, while it is unnecessary to implement every programme component across all regions, there are areas where by doing so, UNDP has helped to bring about coherence across the country.

The previous ADR recommended that UNDP should develop different programme strategies for each region which would allow coherence of the programme across the region. Yet the project of a federal Somalia, which the ADR recognizes is increasingly assuming centre stage, also requires some coherence in approach across all Somali regions, for example the development of a single Somalia police force or judicial system, or a common national strategy to address HIV and AIDS. Yet while the county office faces the challenge of balancing vertical integration across regions with horizontal integration across programmes, it is clear that each region has a very different context.

The relative stability of Somaliland means that it could be used for testing innovative approaches that, if successful, could be replicated in other regions where and when appropriate. It also means, for example, that different approaches could be used for livelihoods support (such as microfinance) or for capacity development, for example more institutionalizing of UNDP efforts compared to the approaches possible in southern and central regions. At the same time, it may be challenging for programme managers situated in Mogadishu not to focus mainly on Mogadishu and it may also take time for programme managers to develop adequate knowledge of the local situation in other regions. Further delegation of authority and responsibility to the regions as well as more decentralized programming could allow a more optimal balance to be achieved.

Conclusion 4. Both the ADR and previous evaluations have found that the UNDP contribution to strengthening national capacities has been less than expected. While sufficient analysis is required to account for the low base from which interventions started, new joint

---

140   The role of good governance in promoting development is contested. See, for example, the discussion in the edited volume, 'Is Good Governance Good for Development?', United Nations Series on Development, 2 October 2012.

initiatives aimed at broad capacity development in the public sector should also recognize past failures and undertake analysis of context-specific constraints and opportunities.

The UNDP contribution to capacity development has been limited. Some good work has been done but it is often fragmented and usually at an individual rather than institutional level. Over the period being examined, there have been many short training sessions and workshops but not all were necessarily useful and sustainable. Evaluations have revealed weaknesses in the SIDP but many of the problems can apply to capacity development work in other areas.

Context matters in capacity development and it can present constraints or opportunities. Building functioning institutions in a weak governance environment is complex and seeing tangible results takes time. The highly evolving operational context which, for example, saw three Prime Ministers in office in as many years entailed frequent turnover of government staff and has hampered institutional capacity development efforts.[141] On the other hand, the formation of the federal states provides opportunities for capacity development at subnational level tailored to local realities. Given weak governance practices such as those in Somalia, there is a need to find a balance between the four core issues identified in the UNDP capacity development framework.[142]

Conclusion 5. UNDP management and staff are committed and receptive to the UNDP gender equality and women's empowerment strategy and the country office has a gender mainstreaming architecture in place. While this is important, UNDP will deliver few gender results if it does not move away from 'soft' support (gender policy, advocacy, lobbying) and

coverage of number of trainees to economic empowerment in terms of technical and business skills.

Some valuable groundwork has been laid in the area of gender equality and women's empowerment. UNDP built strong foundation for gender mainstreaming through planning processes such as developing a gender equality strategy; a 'gender mainstreaming made easy' tool, the Gender Equality Seal, etc. UNDP has also committed financial resources, although without a system in place to track financial expenditures there is no way of monitoring gender-related expenditures. The gender equality programme needs to be strengthened if desired gender results[143] are to be achieved.

Conclusion 6. UNDP monitoring and reporting of results tend to emphasize inputs and immediate outputs with less orientation on intermediate outcome results. This can be linked to several factors: the broad framework of UNDP support, which has to be responsive to Governments; the intangible and difficult-to-measure nature of UNDP support, e.g., strengthening governance systems, capacity development and policy advice; and insufficient institutional capacity (human resources, tools and skills). The corollary for UNDP is the inability to demonstrate its contribution to development results which in turn has consequences for forging effective partnerships and mobilizing resources.

With aid budgets under pressure, there is an urgent need for UNDP to draw on innovations to strengthen monitoring and reporting to meet internal and external accountability, learning and decision-making demands. In a country where for some areas of its work UNDP must

---

141 The incumbent Prime Minister is the third in office since the formation of the Federal Government of Somalia in 2012.

142 The four core issues are institutional arrangements, leadership, knowledge and accountability. Source: UNDP, 'Capacity Development: A UNDP Primer', 2009.

143 Gender results are defined as outputs or outcomes assessed to be contributing (positively or negatively) in UNDP interventions to gender equality and women's empowerment.

act remotely through implementing partners, it is necessary to explore the use of alternative institutional arrangements to strengthen results-based monitoring. UNDP has launched third-party monitoring systems with a follow-up mechanism in place to ensure use of the findings. This practice needs to be institutionalized and sustained. The focus of monitoring should also shift from tracking mere numbers to intermediate results.

6.2 RECOMMENDATIONS

Since the main purpose of the ADR is to inform the development of a new country programme, most of the recommendations are at a strategic level. Others can be implemented immediately, for example recommendation 5 related to strengthening monitoring and evaluation. Some of the recommendations call for a review of the situation, which is not to imply that the project staff may not be aware of the issues that need to be addressed, but rather an attempt to document knowledge for potential sharing and use including outside of the country office.

Recommendation 1: Recognizing the complexity and fluidity of the Somali context, the ADR recommends that UNDP Somalia, in developing its new country programme, should continue to pursue an adaptive planning and management approach.

The validity of medium- to long-term planning approaches in a high-risk environment characterized by rapidly changing political, security and humanitarian situations such as Somalia's merits closer examination. The planning and management of the programme, including decisions on staff relocation, should remain flexible enough to allow for progressive elaboration of strategies and short-term results and targets based on newly emerging developments. Somalia will be holding parliamentary and presidential elections in 2016. A national development plan will also be developed which will come into effect in 2017. The country office should use the best available expertise and technical support from within and outside UNDP to design a new country programme that is adaptable to changing conditions and balances between Somalia's short-term and long-term development needs.

Management response: UNDP Somalia agrees with this recommendation. UNDP has maintained its flexibility to the Somali context by: (a) aligning its programmes to the New Deal priorities and the PSGs, and by designing and aligning new programmes under the Compact aid architecture/ SDRF; (b) expanding its portfolio specifically to support key political priorities, including electoral support, review of the Constitution and support to newly emerging federal states, focusing on both the short-term political deliverables and on building institutional capacity for longer-term democratic development in Somalia; (c) expanding its institutional support to governance institutions such as parliaments in the newly emerging federal states; (d) developing a comprehensive youth employment strategy and joint programme to support the long-term employability of Somali youth through strengthening of value chains in key growth sectors; and (e) rolling out new programming to support climate change resilience at community level.

UNDP Somalia is currently supporting the Federal Government to prepare its first NDP in more than two decades, in order to focus future development interventions on poverty reduction and addressing the root causes of vulnerability that underlie the volatile humanitarian context, while maintaining an integrated focus on the intersection between politics, security and development. UNDP will develop its next country programme in alignment with the new NDP. The future country programme will reiterate the need for flexibility with regard to immediate priorities while also maintaining a commitment to longer-term development objectives and the Sustainable Development Goals.

Recommendation 2: UNDP Somalia should recalibrate the profile of the poverty reduction and environment programme if it is to meet the immediate and long-term needs of the vulnerable population.

One of the approaches which UNDP Somalia successfully pursued to increase the coverage of the poverty reduction programme is mainstreaming and promoting synergies among programme components, as noted above. Another viable strategy that the office should explore is reallocating regular resources from some of the programme components with dependable flows of other resources to poverty reduction. UNDP Somalia should conduct a strategic review of the programme to document past good performance and lessons learned with a view to developing bankable projects that can persuade donors to fund UNDP.

Management response: The country office is in broad agreement with the recommendation. The country office's programmatic portfolio on poverty reduction and resilience has been expanding rapidly. Key new projects include the joint programme on youth employment (2015–2018), with UN-Habitat, ILO and FAO; the joint programme for sustainable charcoal reduction and alternative livelihoods, with FAO and UNEP; and the Global Environment Facility-funded project on enhancing climate resilience of the vulnerable communities and ecosystems in Somalia (2015-2018). The country office is working with the UNCT to develop a new joint programme on durable solutions to displacement in Somalia with UN-Habitat and the Office of the United Nations High Commissioner for Refugees (UNHCR), and new initiatives related to renewable energy, climate-smart approaches to rural development and local economic development.

However, the country office recognizes the need for a forward-looking review of the poverty reduction and environment programme with a focus on longer-term poverty reduction, including shifting from short-term employment to longer-term employment at scale, particularly for youth and women, that will drive economic growth and support overall stability. The new NDP will provide a key opportunity for UNDP to reposition its work – and its engagement with the Government and donor partners – in favour of a greater focus on poverty reduction, and a strategic review as suggested would likewise assist in this respect.

The comments on regular resources are well noted. Regular resources have played a critical role in initiating new programmes, and in bridging gaps when donor funding is sometimes unpredictable. A flexible approach to TRAC allocations is therefore necessary.

Recommendation 3: There is a need to review the current approach to capacity development in the country programme and to devise a conceptual framework for more effective and sustainable capacity development across the board.

The evaluation found that short-term training without follow-up remained the main component of most capacity development efforts during the period under review. Somalia needs a comprehensive human resources development strategy informed by the context. The new joint programme should not become a 'vertical' programme but ensure that capacity development is cross-cutting and builds on emerging opportunities, such as the formation of states (federalism) which may provide new opportunities for capacity development at subnational levels. Notwithstanding declining donor funds, UNDP should advocate for and strive to balance capacity development needs of the Federal Government and the emerging federal states if there is to be a cohesive government structure.

Management response: The country office is in broad agreement with the recommendation. The findings of the ADR concerning the often limited impact of capacity development efforts were recognized and led to the development of a new capacity development programme during 2014 and the beginning of 2015, consisting of two main projects: strengthening institutional performance, working on the federal level and in Puntland; and the state formation project, working in the emerging states. Both projects became operational during 2015. These are in addition to longstanding support to district governments through the joint programme on local governance, which is now being expanded to new districts in the south of the country.

Improvements in the country office's overall approach to capacity development are taking place on three levels:

- ***Focusing capacity development towards core government functions,*** *including planning, monitoring, evaluation and statistics; organizational structures and functional arrangements on vertical and horizontal levels; internal and external coordination mechanisms; civil service management, with a strong focus on human resource management; administrative management (including financial, personnel, office systems, etc.); policy and strategy development (systemic improvements); and gender mainstreaming in selected key areas;*

- ***Focusing capacity development support on the internal capacities of supporting institutions,*** *in line with the overall UNDP approach to capacity development, with its focus on organizational development, and directly linked to the HACT capacity assessments and functional reviews undertaken. The support provided to government institutions focuses on strengthening internal systems of governance as well as the individual capacities of staff members to discharge their functions; organizational reforms; regulatory development; designing terms of reference; and classic training of the supporting institutions' staff;*

- ***Stimulating consistency in the capacity development approach throughout the country programme.*** *While specific capacity development projects are being delivered at federal, state and district levels, as noted above, capacity development is an important and cross-cutting element of all UNDP-supported projects. Steps have been taken to further harmonize the capacity development approach and stimulate a higher level of coherence in the country programme. This element, however, does require more attention, and will be taken forward through the formulation of the new country programme, which is likely to occur towards the end of 2016, bringing the overall programme structure in line with the expectations of the forthcoming NDP.*

Recommendation 4: UNDP should prioritize substantive gender mainstreaming in the next country programme.

The decision by senior management to include the gender adviser as member of the senior management team is promising but linkages should be strengthened with programme and operations staff. UNDP should also explore and strengthen alternative strategic partnerships, including with other United Nations agencies, donors, academia, media, etc. to go beyond traditional roles as funders and implementers and to foster new partnerships and forums which advance gender equality; for example, partnerships with social and alternative media organizations as a vehicle to engage young men and women on gender concerns. UNDP should also advocate for gender representation in the PSG technical working groups and High-Level Partnership Forum to ensure gender-responsive policy and programmatic decisions and monitoring and evaluation.

Management response: UNDP Somalia agrees with this recommendation. The CPD for 2011-2016 had a dedicated gender-specific outcome and provided a framework within which to implement the corporate mandate of gender mainstreaming across all country programme outcomes. The country office has made efforts and progress in consolidating past gains, building on lessons learned and drawing inspiration from corporate commitments to gender equality and women's empowerment, as reflected in the Gender Equality Seal High Silver award which the country office received in 2015. Recommendations from the Gender Equality Seal process are now being implemented, in order to progress towards a target of Gold. The country office, together with other UNCT members, has supported gender representation in the Somali Compact processes, including two side-events on women and gender equity issues at the High-Level Partnership Forums in 2015 and 2016. To attain even further results in terms of gender mainstreaming, the country office will focus on the following:

a) *Mainstreaming gender empowerment and women's empowerment in the next country programme;*

b) *Continued delivery of specific initiatives to advance gender empowerment and women's empowerment, including on women's political participation, the gender dimension of the NDP and Sustainable Development Goal 5;*

c) *Building and strengthening strategic partnerships to increase the impact of efforts to promote gender empowerment and women's empowerment, as recommended by the ADR;*

d) *Improving gender-responsive planning, monitoring, reporting and evaluation.*

Recommendation 5: UNDP should increase investments to enhance internal monitoring and reporting capacities. It is encouraging that UNDP has already initiated alternative institutional arrangements to strengthen results-based monitoring and reporting, such as third-party monitoring in 2015. Capacities of implementing partners to monitor their work during implementation and ex-post should also be assessed and strengthened as part of broader capacity development efforts.

Given that the ability of UNDP Somalia staff to monitor programme implementation is curtailed by insecurity, inaccessibility and other constraints, the engagement by UNDP of an institution for third-party monitoring in early 2015 is a positive step. The office is also cognizant that the focus of such monitoring must move away from mere numbers and attempt to highlight the contribution of UNDP to intermediate results.

UNDP should continue to identify internal learning needs in relation to results-based monitoring and reporting. Repeated training opportunities including both formal training and on-the-job orientation are needed since one-off results-based management training is not sufficient to improve skills. Strengthening nascent national monitoring and reporting capacities is also relevant as the country prepares its post-Vision 2016 national development framework. Some of these efforts can build on ongoing initiatives such as the rolling out the HACT and must move away from compliance-based capacity development.

Management response: UNDP Somalia agrees with this recommendation. The country office has strengthened internal monitoring and reporting through a number of means, including increasing the number of national M&E staff in projects and in the Programme and Planning Unit. The third-party monitoring arrangements in place not only verify numbers or activities, but also seek more output- and outcome-related results, including beneficiary satisfaction and project effectiveness, among others. All project documents, annual workplans and partnership agreements are reviewed by the M&E team prior to approval. Similarly, all implementation arrangements (letters of agreement, grants, etc.) are scrutinized through the Local Project Appraisal Committee, to ensure that proper capacity assessment and appropriate risk mitigation measures have been put in place. The letters of agreement and grant agreements also contain requirements for improved partner reporting, third-party monitoring as commissioned by UNDP and provision of beneficiary contacts in order to conduct follow-up verification. The office has revised its reporting templates with a focus on evidence-based reporting and inclusion of monitoring and oversight activities.

In 2016, the country office will continue to develop these arrangements. Work is ongoing to deepen capacity development of national counterparts specifically in the areas of results- based management and reporting. This includes specific support, for instance, to the new M&E team at the Ministry of Planning and International Cooperation on results-based management and monitoring of progress towards the Sustainable Development Goals, and on the preparation of the monitoring framework for the new NDP. The country office will continue these efforts through devising a feedback mechanism for senior management on monitoring findings and follow-up actions; expanded capacity development of national partners on results-based management and reporting; establishment of a country office M&E working group for national staff; tracking frequency of monitoring visits undertaken by project and programme staff; and using social media to inform stakeholders of third-party monitoring findings.

 CHAPTER 6. CONCLUSIONS AND RECOMMENDATIONS

TERMS OF REFERENCE

1. INTRODUCTION

The Independent Evaluation Office (IEO) of the United Nations Development Program (UNDP) conducts country evaluations called "Assessments of Development Results" (ADRs) to capture and demonstrate evaluative evidence of UNDP's contributions to development results at the country level, as well as the effectiveness of UNDP's strategy in facilitating and leveraging national effort for achieving development results. The purpose of an ADR is to:

- Provide substantive support to the Administrator's accountability function in reporting to the Executive Board.

- Support greater UNDP accountability to national stakeholders and partners in the programme country.

- Serve as a means of quality assurance for UNDP interventions at the country level.

- Contribute to learning at corporate, regional and country levels.

ADRs are independent evaluations carried out within the overall provisions contained in the UNDP Evaluation Policy.[144] The IEO is independent of UNDP management and is headed by a Director who reports to the UNDP Executive Board. The responsibility of the IEO is two-fold: (a) provide the Executive Board with valid and credible information from evaluations for corporate accountability, decision-making and improvement; and (b) enhance the independence, credibility and utility of the evaluation function, and its coherence, harmonization and alignment in support of United Nations reform and national ownership. Based on the principle of national ownership, IEO seeks to conduct ADRs in collaboration with the national authorities where the country programme is implemented.

The first ADR for Somalia was conducted in 2010 and covered the period 2005 to 2010. This second ADR will be conducted in 2014 with a view to contributing to the realignment of the ongoing country programme (2011-2015) and the corresponding gender strategy to ensure consistency with:

- the Somali New Deal Compact;

- the United Nations Integrated Strategic Framework;

- the UNDP Strategic Plan, 2014-2017 and gender equality strategy, 2014-2017[145] In so doing, the ADR will also contribute to the preparation of the new UNDP country programme that will begin in 2017.[146]

---

144   See UNDP Evaluation Policy: www.undp.org/eo/documents/Evaluation-Policy.pdf. The ADR will also be conducted in adherence to the Norms and the Standards and the ethical Code of Conduct established by the United Nations Evaluation Group (www.uneval.org).

145   The UNDP gender strategy 2014-2017 provides detailed guidance for UNDP business units on how to mainstream gender perspectives as they operationalize all aspects of the UNDP Strategic Plan, 2014-2017. This includes identifying strategic entry points for advancing gender equality and women's empowerment in all seven outcomes of the Strategic Plan.

146   The country office will seek a one-year extension of the ongoing 2011-2015 programme.

2. NATIONAL CONTEXT

Much of Somalia's recent past has been market by poverty, famine and recurring violence. The 2013 report on the Millennium Development Goals suggest that Somalia is unlikely to achieve 19 of the 20 targets examined in the report. With more than 70 per cent of the population under the age of 30, Somalia is a young country with enormous development needs.

When the current UNDP country programme document was designed (late 2009) there was a very different political situation than today. After eight years of transition, the Transitional Federal Government formed in 2004 ended on 10 September 2012 with the adoption of a new Provisional Constitution, formation of a new Parliament and the selection of a President. With the completion of the transition, the United Nations established a new political mission led by the United Nations Department of Political Affairs, the United Nations Assistance Mission in Somalia (UNSOM) replacing the United Nations Political Office for Somalia (UNPOS).

On 16 September 2013 a conference on establishing a New Deal for Somalia was held in Brussels, co-hosted by the Somali Federal Government and the European Union. The conference endorsed a New Deal Compact between the Government and the international community that will guide the reconstruction of Somalia. The Compact sets out the priorities for Somalia to attain long-term peacebuilding and State-building outcomes as set out in five Peace and State-Building Goals (PSGs): inclusive politics, security, justice, economic foundations, and revenues and services. Gender perspectives are integrated into the body of the Compact including the need to take into account the specific needs of women and girls in each PSG. The United Nations is now developing an Integrated Strategic Framework to coordinate its work in support of the Compact.

The constantly shifting and rapidly evolving political landscape in Somalia necessitates adjustments and forging new partnerships. This presents equally complex challenges and makes implementation of long- term plans extremely difficult. In addition to the challenge of the complex and insecure working environment in which it works, UNDP in Somalia suffered a number of disruptions in the first three years of implementing the ongoing country programme:

On 20 July 2011, the United Nations officially declared famine in two regions in the southern part of Somalia and by August, 4 million people were in crisis and 750,000 people were at a risk of starvation and living in famine conditions.

In 2012 UNDP started the process of formally moving the country office from Nairobi to Mogadishu and by the end of the year the country director had been relocated there. This was disruptive for both national and international staff.

On 19 June 2013, terrorists attacked the United Nations Common Compound in Mogadishu and UNDP personnel were among the casualties. This resulted in the move of the key staff members, including senior management, back to Nairobi. A decision has now been made to return to Mogadishu and a phased relocation will begin end-April 2014.

3. UNDP PROGRAMME STRATEGY IN SOMALIA

The UNDP country programme was approved by the UNDP Executive Board at the second regular session of 2010. The programme was expected to contribute to four broad outcomes as illustrated in table 1.

The country programme is divided into three subprogrammes: (a) governance and rule of law; (b) poverty reduction and environmental protection; and (c) gender (both a programme and a cross-cutting issue). HIV and AIDS and peace and Security are also considered cross-cutting issues. The relationship between these programmes and the four country programme

Country programme outcome		Indicative resources (Millions of US$)
Outcome 1	Somali women and men and authorities are better able to build peace and manage conflict.	13.5
Outcome 2	Somali women and men, girls and boys benefit from more inclusive, equitable and accountable governance, improved services, human security, access to justice and human rights.	110.75
Outcome 3	Somali women and men benefit from increased sustainable livelihood opportunities and improved natural resources management.	83.3
Outcome 4	Somali women and men attain greater gender equality and are empowered.	12.45
	Total	220

Source: UNDP Somalia country programme document, 2011-2015 (DP/DCP/SOM/2)

Table A2. Outcomes, programmes and cross-cutting issues

Outcomes	Programmes	Programme components	Cross-cutting		
1	Governance and rule of law	• Local governance • Institutional development • Constitutional reform and parliament	Gender	HIV and AIDS	Peace and security
2		• Civilian police • Access to justice • Community security			
3	Poverty reduction and environmental protection	• Private sector development • Local economic development • Human development/Millennium Development Goals • Environmental management			
4	Gender				

Source: Interviews with country office staff/annual report

outcomes is illustrated in table 2, which also sets out the components of the programmes.

4. SCOPE OF THE EVALUATION

Since the first Somalia ADR covered the country programme 2005 to 2010, this evaluation will only cover UNDP initiatives undertaken under the first three years of the ongoing country programme, 2011 to 2015. The evaluation is both retrospective and prospective. Retrospectively, the ADR will assess the UNDP contribution to national efforts aimed at addressing development challenges and

provide conclusions on the overall performance of UNDP. It will assess key results, anticipated and unanticipated, positive and negative, and will cover UNDP assistance funded from both regular and other resources. The evaluation will also examine the contribution of the country office gender strategy (2012–2015) which is aligned to the country programme, to achieving gender results within UNDP development support to Somalia. Based on the findings from the assessment of past performance, the evaluation will look ahead to examine how UNDP can become better aligned to the various instruments outlined in section 1 as well as better strategically positioned to increase its development contribution. Special efforts will be made to look at operational and management issues and how they have affected this contribution.

5. METHODOLOGY

The evaluation has two main components: (a) the analysis of the UNDP contribution to development results (specifically, against the outcomes contained in the country programme document); and (b) the strategy UNDP has adopted to enhance contribution to development results in Somalia. For each component, the ADR will present its findings and assessment according to the set criteria provided below. Further elaboration of the criteria will be found in *ADR Manual 2011*. Evaluators assess the programmes against the criteria, generate findings and come to broad conclusions from the evaluation to draw recommendations for future action.

- **The UNDP contribution by thematic/programmatic areas.** Analysis will be made of the contribution of UNDP to development results of Somalia through its programme activities. The analysis will be presented by outcome areas and according to the following criteria:

  - **Relevance** of UNDP projects and outcomes to the country's needs and national priorities;

  - **Effectiveness** of UNDP interventions in terms of achieving intended programme outcomes;

  - **Efficiency** of UNDP interventions in terms of use of human and financial resources; and

  - **Sustainability** of the results to which UNDP contributed.

- **The UNDP contribution through its strategic positioning.** The positioning and strategies of UNDP are analysed both from the perspective of the organization's mandate and the development needs and priorities in the country as agreed and as they emerged. This will entail systematic analysis of the UNDP position within the development and policy space in the country, as well as strategies used by UNDP to maximize its contribution through adopting relevant strategies and approaches. The following criteria will be applied:

  - **Relevance and responsiveness** of the county programme as a whole to the challenges and needs of the country;

  - Use of the comparative **strengths** of UNDP;

  - Promoting **United Nations values** from human development perspective.

Specific attention will be paid to UNDP support to **furthering gender equality and women's empowerment** in Somalia in agreement with the UN SWAP.[147] The evaluation will systematically assess how gender is mainstreamed in the overall programme support of UNDP, and how direct gender-related interventions helped to further gender equality and women's empowerment.

The evaluation criteria form the basis of the ADR methodological process. In addition to assessments made using the criteria above, the ADR process will also identify how various factors can explain the performance of UNDP. Factors that will be considered in this ADR are:

- National context, political environment, conflict and security;

- National ownership of initiatives and results and use of national capacities;

- Gender equality and women's empowerment as preconditions for sustainable human development;

---

147 United Nations System-wide Action Plan on Gender Equality and the Empowerment of Women, http://www.unwomen.org/~/media/Headquarters/Attachments/Sections/How%20We%20Work/UNSystemCoordination/UN-SWAP-Framework-Dec-2012.pdf

- South-South solutions and cooperation;

- Management, including programme management, human resources management and financial management.

In addition, the evaluation will also examine a number of other factors that are assumed to have had an impact on the performance of UNDP over the last three years:

- The implications of the relocation of staff, including senior management, to and from Mogadishu;

- Security issues and associated limitations to implementation (including monitoring);

- Selection of implementation modalities and monitoring in the context of remote management;

- Gender perspectives of the country office business environment;

- The role in the integrated mission, coordination issues and joint work;

- Support from headquarters (RBAS, BDP and BCPR) and the Regional Service Centre.

An outcome paper will be developed for each outcome noted in table 1 above, which examines the programme's progress towards the respective outcome and the UNDP contribution to that change since 2011. A theory of change[148] approach will be used and developed by the evaluation team in consultation with UNDP and national stakeholders. Discussions of the theory of change will focus on mapping the assumptions made about a programme's desired change and causal linkages expected and these will form a basis for the data collection approach that will verify the theories behind the changes found. The outcome papers will use the theory of change approach to assess the UNDP contribution to the outcome using the evaluation criteria, and identify the factors that have influenced this contribution. Each outcome paper will be prepared according to a standard template provided by the IEO which will facilitate synthesis and the identification of conclusions and recommendations in the ADR report for UNDP to consider together with main partners for future programming.

The evaluation will take into account the fact that although the projects are centrally managed, there are different elements implemented in each of the areas covered by the Mogadishu country office and the two sub-offices in Garowe and Hargeisa. Efforts will be made to make separate assessments for each of these areas as well as for the overall programme.

6. DATA COLLECTION

Assessment of data collection constraints and existing data. An assessment was carried for each outcome to ascertain the available information and identify data constraints to determine the data collection needs and method. The assessment outlined the level of evaluable data that is available. The assessment indicates that: (a) six evaluations were commissioned by the country office since the start of the 2011-2015 country programme with four completed[149] and

---

148 "Theory of Change is an outcome-based approach which applies critical thinking to the design, implementation and evaluation of initiatives and programmes intended to support change in their contexts. While there is no single definition and set methodology, at a critical minimum, theory of change is considered to encompass discussion of the following elements:

- Context for the initiative, including social, political and environmental conditions; Long-term change that the initiative seeks to support and for whose ultimate benefit; Process/sequence of change anticipated to lead to the desired long-term outcome;

- Assumptions about how these changes might happen, as a check on whether the activities and outputs are appropriate for influencing change in the desired direction in this context; Diagram and narrative summary that captures the outcome of the discussion.

Source: Vogel, Isabel, 'Review of the use of 'Theory of Change' in International Development', April 2012, DFID.

149 Completed and uploaded onto the UNDP Evaluation Resource Centre.

two more to be complete in time for use by the ADR.[150] Although there are no outcome evaluations, Somalia has been a case study in two recent evaluations commissioned by the Bureau for Crisis Prevention and Recovery;[151] (b) systematic monitoring of outcomes is available for the evaluation to build on; and (c) monitoring of outputs has sometimes been challenging due to security reasons. The data collection methods and tools aim to address the data gaps, as well as the policy-level information not covered in existing evaluations.

Data collection methods. The evaluation will use data from primary and secondary sources, including desk review of documentation and information and interviews with key informants, including beneficiaries, partners and managers. Specific evaluation questions for each criteria and the data collection method will be further detailed and outlined in the outcome papers. A multi-stakeholder approach will be followed and interviews will include government representatives, civil society organizations, private sector representatives, United Nations agencies, multilateral organizations, bilateral donors, and beneficiaries of the programme. Focus groups will be used to consult some groups of beneficiaries as appropriate.

The criteria for selecting places for field visits include: accessibility/security; critical mass of project interventions; potential for significant learning (both successful as well as challenging cases); and coverage of all programme areas.

The IEO and the country office have identified an initial list of background and programme-related documents which is posted on an ADR SharePoint website. The following secondary data will be reviewed: background documents on the national context, documents prepared by international partners during the period under review and documents prepared by United Nations system agencies; programme plans and frameworks; progress reports; monitoring self-assessments such as the UNDP results-oriented annual report; and evaluations conducted by the country office and partners. The ADR will also support, where possible and appropriate, the ongoing data collection endeavours being undertaken by UNDP projects for outcome monitoring.

Validation. The evaluation will use triangulation of information collected from different sources and/or by different methods to ensure that the data is valid.

Stakeholder involvement: At the start of the evaluation, a stakeholder analysis was conducted to identify all relevant UNDP partners, as well as those who may not work with UNDP but play a key role in the outcomes to which UNDP contributes. To the extent possible, the evaluation will use a participatory approach to the design, implementation and reporting of the ADR.

7. MANAGEMENT ARRANGEMENTS

Independent Evaluation Office of UNDP: The UNDP IEO will conduct the ADR in consultation with the Somalia country office, the Regional Bureau for Arab States and the Somali Federal Government.[152] The IEO evaluation managers will lead the evaluation and coordinate the evaluation team. The IEO will meet all costs directly related to the conduct of the ADR.

Federal Government of Somalia: The Federal Government of Somalia and other key government counterparts of UNDP in Somalia will facilitate the conduct of ADR by: providing necessary access to information sources within the government; safeguarding the independence of the evaluation; and jointly organizing the final stakeholder meeting with the IEO when it is

---

150 Somali Institutional Development Project (SIDP) and joint programme on local governance.

151 UNDP reintegration programmes and UNDP-supported mobile courts interventions.

152 Where reference is made to the Federal Government of Somalia, the evaluation also recognizes the Somaliland Special Arrangement as set out in the New Deal Compact

ANNEX 1. TERMS OF REFERENCE

time to present findings and results of the evaluation. Additionally, the counterparts will be responsible within the Federal Government of Somalia for the use and dissemination of the final outputs of the ADR process.

UNDP country office in Somalia: The country office will support the evaluation team to liaise with key partners and other stakeholders, make available to the team all necessary information regarding UNDP programmes, projects and activities in the country, and provide factual verifications of the draft report on a timely basis. The country office (and the sub-offices) will provide the evaluation team support in kind (e.g., arranging meetings with project staff, stakeholders and beneficiaries; and assistance for the project site visits). To ensure the independence of the views expressed in interviews and meetings with stakeholders held for data collection purposes, country office staff will not participate.

UNDP Regional Bureau for Arab States: The UNDP Regional Bureau for Arab States will support the evaluation through information-sharing and will also participate in discussions on emerging conclusions and recommendations.

Reference Group: Three reference groups will be established representing the three areas covered by the UNDP sub-offices. The groups will comprise national and international partners as appropriate and will be responsible for reviewing the terms of reference (ToR) and the draft report.

Evaluation Team: The IEO will constitute an evaluation team to undertake the ADR. The IEO will ensure gender balance in the team which will include the following members:

1. **Evaluation Manager (EM)**, The EM has the overall responsibility for managing the ADR, and will

   - prepare and design the evaluation (i.e., this ToR);

   - select the evaluation team and provide methodological guidance.

The evaluation manager will cover the portion of the evaluation related to

- strategic positioning issues;

- coordination issues;

- preparation of reports for outcomes 1 and 2 covered by the governance and rule of law programme;

- the synthesis process;

- preparation of the draft and final reports.

The EM will travel to Nairobi, Mogadishu and one of the two sub-offices in Somalia

2. **Associate Evaluation Manager (AEM):** The AEM will support the EM in:

   - preparation and design of the evaluation;

   - the selection of the evaluation team;

   - undertake synthesis with EM;

   - review draft report;

   - other aspects of the ADR process as may be required.

Specifically, the AEM will oversee data collection and analysis for the poverty reduction and environment programme outcome (#3) and prepare the outcome report. The AEM will visit Nairobi, Mogadishu and one of the two sub-offices in Somalia.

3. **Senior Strategic Consultant:** The senior strategic consultant is responsible for supporting the evaluation team's analysis of the strategic positioning of UNDP in Somalia. Specifically, the Senior Strategic Consultant will:

   - Review early drafts of the ADR report and outcome papers;

   - Join the data synthesis process.

4. **Operations Specialist (OS):** The operations specialist will examine operational and management issues and identify how they have affected the UNDP contribution to development results over the last three years.

5. **Gender Specialist (GS)**: The gender specialist is responsible for evaluating the UNDP contribution to gender equality and women's empowerment since the start of 2011. Specifically, he/she will:

- review the UNDP gender strategy, project documents, monitoring systems, reports, etc. to assess if gender has been effectively mainstreamed;

- Review the country office business environment from a gender perspective;

- Collect data from gender projects in two subregions and ensure the data collection team (below) can address gender issues in its work;

- Prepare an outcome paper for country programme outcome 4 and review other three outcome reports to ensure gender addressed adequately;

- Join the data synthesis process;

- Review the draft ADR report to ensure gender addressed adequately.

6. **Data collection team**: The data collection team is responsible for collecting data on the performance of UNDP interventions since 2011 in the three subregions of Somalia. Specifically, the team will be responsible for:

- Reviewing project documentation prior to field work;

- Visiting three project sites in each of the three areas of each subregion;

- Validating self-reporting of results and identify factors affecting performance;

- Preparing reports on findings.

7. **Research Assistant**: A research assistant based in the IEO will provide background research and documentation.

8. EVALUATION PROCESS

The evaluation will be conducted according to the approved IEO process as outlined in the ADR Manual. The following represents a summary of key elements of the process. Four major phases provide a framework conducting the evaluation.

Phase 1: Preparation. The IEO prepares the ToR and the evaluation design, following a preparatory mission to UNDP Somalia office located in Nairobi by the Evaluation Manager. The preparatory mission to Nairobi, and discussions with UNDP programme staff, include the following objectives:

- ensure that key country office staff are familiar with the objectives of the ADR and the ADR process;

- gain a much stronger understanding of the country programme, its origins, the country office's strategies, etc.;

- understand the intended use of evaluation;

Table A3. Data collection responsibilities by outcome		
Outcome	**Report**	**Data collection**
Outcome 1	EM	EM and data collectors
Outcome 2	EM	EM and data collectors
Outcome 3	AEM	AEM and data collectors
Outcome 4	GS	GS and data collectors
HIV and AIDS	EM	EM and data collectors
Strategic positioning issues	—	EM, GS, AEM and senior strategic consultant
Operations and management issues	OS	OS, EM and GS

- assess the programme evaluability prior to developing the ToR;

- understand the logistical and practical constraints when evaluating a remotely managed programme with three separate sub-regions in a poor security context;

- identify companies that could help with data collection in Somalia;

- identify areas where support can be provided for ongoing data collection endeavours being undertaken by UNDP projects for outcome monitoring.

Additional evaluation team members, comprising international and/or national development professionals, will be recruited once the ToR is complete.

Phase 2: Data collection and analysis. The phase will commence in late May 2014. An evaluation matrix with detailed questions and means of data collection and verification will be developed to guide data collection. The following process will be undertaken:

- pre-mission activities: Evaluation team members conduct desk reviews of reference material, and prepare a summary of the context and other evaluative evidence, and identify the outcome theory of change, outcome-specific evaluation questions, gaps and issues that will require validation during the field-based phase of data collection;

- data collection mission: The evaluation team will undertake a mission to the country to engage in data collection activities. The estimated duration of the mission is a total of three weeks in late May/early June. Data will be collected according to the approach outlined in section 6 with responsibilities outlined in section 7.

Phase 3: Synthesis, report writing and review. Based on the outcome reports, the EM, AEM, GS and senior strategic consultant will undertake a synthesis process.

The first draft of the ADR report will be prepared and subjected to the quality control process of the IEO. Once cleared by the IEO, the first draft will be further circulated with the country office and the Regional Bureau for Arab States for factual corrections. The second draft, which takes into account factual corrections, will be shared with national stakeholders for review.

The draft report will then be shared at stakeholder workshop where the results of the evaluation will be presented to key national stakeholders. Moreover, the ways forward will be discussed with a view to creating greater ownership by national stakeholders in taking forward the lessons and recommendations from the report, and to strengthening accountability of UNDP to national stakeholders. Taking into account the discussion at the stakeholder workshops, the final evaluation report will be prepared. The UNDP Somalia country office will prepare the management response to the ADR, under the oversight of RBAS.

Phase 4: Production, dissemination and follow-up. The ADR report and brief will be widely distributed in both hard and electronic versions. The evaluation report will be made available to the UNDP Executive Board by the time of approving a new country programme document. It will be widely distributed by the IEO within UNDP as well as to the evaluation units of other international organizations, evaluation societies/networks and research institutions in the region. The Somalia country office and Federal Government of Somalia will disseminate to stakeholders in the country. The report and the management response will be published on the UNDP website[153] as well as in the Evaluation Resource Centre. RBAS will be responsible for monitoring and overseeing the implementation of follow-up actions in the Evaluation Resource Centre.[154]

---

153   www.undp.org/eo/

154   http://erc.undp.org/

9.   TIMEFRAME FOR THE ADR PROCESS[155]

The timeframe and responsibilities for the evaluation process are tentatively as follows:

Table A4: Timeframe for the ADR process		
Activity	**Responsible**	**Proposed timeframe**
Phase 1: Preparation		
Preparatory mission	EM	March 2014
ToR – approval by the Independent Evaluation Office	EM	April
Selection of other evaluation team members	EM and AEM	April
Phase 2: Data collection and analysis		
Preliminary analysis of available data and context analysis	Evaluation team	April
Data collection analysis, outcome reports drafting,	Evaluation team	May/June 2014
Phase 3: Synthesis and report writing		
Synthesis	EM, GS and AEM	July
Zero draft ADR for clearance by IEO	EM	July
First draft ADR for country office/RBAS review	EM	July
Second Draft for national reference group review	EM	August
Stakeholder Workshop	IEO, country office, Federal Government of Somalia	November
Phase 4: Production and Follow-up		
Editing and formatting	IEO	December
Final report and Evaluation Brief	IEO	January 2015
Management response	Country Office	February
Dissemination of the final report	IEO, country office, Federal Government of Somalia	February

---

155   The above timeframe is indicative of the process and deadlines, and does not imply full-time engagement of the evaluation team during the period.

LIST OF PEOPLE CONSULTED

UNDP

NEW YORK

Clapp, David, UNDP Bureau of Management Services/Office of Human Resources (former Country Director, UNDP Somalia)

Lanzoni, Marta, Programme Analyst, UNDP Regional Bureau for Arab States

Nehmeh, Karima, Programme Adviser, UNDP Regional Bureau for Arab States

Rodrigues, Charmaine, Crisis Governance Programme Specialist, UNDP Bureau for Crisis Prevention and Recovery

Shalabi, Asmaa, Programme Specialist, Country Support Management Team, UNDP Bureau for Crisis Prevention and Recovery

Venancio, Moises, Country Adviser, Gulf and Somalia, UNDP Regional Bureau for Arab States

Wahba, Murad, Deputy Director, UNDP Regional Bureau for Arab States

NAIROBI AND MOGADISHU

Aden, Abdirisak Hussein, Project Officer, Poverty Reduction and Environment

Akopyan, David, Deputy Country Director (Programmes)

Al Hammal, Ahmad, Assistant Country Director and Head of Partnerships and Planning Unit

Barre, Mohamed, Programme Specialist of Poverty Reduction and Environment Protection

Brooke, Jonathan, Head of the Poverty Reduction and Environment (based in Mogadishu)

Buzanski, Marcin, Project Manager a.i. Support to Parliament and Constitution Review Project

Byrne, Catriona, Programme Specialist of HIV/AIDS, Programme and Planning Unit

Chudasama, Niraj, Security Associate

Conway, George, Country Director

Diamond, Marie, Former Deputy Country Director

Fowler, Christine, Programme Specialist of Governance and Rule of Law

Freudenberg, Michael, Senior Economist Adviser

Hassan, Bushra, Monitoring and Evaluation Specialist, Partnerships and Planning Unit

Hussain, Mo, Governance Specialist

Janazreh, Kayed, Project Manager of Employment Generation for Early Recovery (based in Garowe, Puntland)

Khojimatov, Sukhrob, Deputy Country Director (Operations)

Musse, Mohamed Barre, Economist (Millennium Development Goal reporting)

Nwogu, Victoria, Gender Specialist and Head of Gender Unit

Pfleiderer, Ruth, Programme Specialist, HIV&AIDS

Rafiq, Abdul Qadire, Protection Manager of Environment and Energy, Poverty Reduction and Environment Protection, Programme and Planning Unit

Ridley, Simon, Project Manager of Access to Justice

Sanchez, Franco, Programme Manager of Governance and Rule of Law

Schumicky-Logan, Lilla, Project Manager
Community Security

James Nunan, Access to Justice Project Manager

Peter Faulhaber, UNDP Civilian Police Project
Manager

Abdullahi, Sahal, Joint Programme on Local
Governance National Project Officer

Ali, Masoud, Programme Associate

Egeh, Bihi, Gender Focal Point

Hussein, Abdullahi, Area Manager for Private
Sector Development Project, Poverty
Reduction and Environment

Kinloch Pichat, Stephen, Head of Sub-office,
Hargeisa (Somaliland)

Mihile, Ahmed, Poverty Reduction and
Environment

Udaya, De Silva, Area Project Manager and
Special Police Unit Adviser of Civilian
Police Project

Yasin, Amren, Programme Specialist

Yusuf, Abdi Abokor, Programme officer of the
Poverty Reduction and Environment

Baker, Amir, Employment Generation for Early
Recovery project manager

Hassan, Abdurazak Mohamed, Joint
Programme on Local Governance National
Programme Officer

Janazreh, Kayed, Poverty Reduction and
Environment Area Manager and Local
Economic Development Project Manager

Mardini, George, International Expert, SIDP

Matatov, Andrey, Area Project Manager,
Civilian Police Project

Nor, Awil Abdi, Community Security National
Project Officer

Sahibzada, Sayed, Head of Garowe Sub-office

Salim, Salim Said, Access to Justice National
Programme Officer

Islan, Nasra, National Programme Officer of
Gender Unit

Yousuf, Mohamed, Programme Specialist,
Programme and Planning Unit

NAIROBI DEVELOPMENT PARTNERS

Clar, Juan, Political-Economic Officer, United
States Embassy, Nairobi

Dahlman, Christina, Senior Programme
Manager, Somalia Section, Embassy of
Sweden

Gacugia, Dorcas, Embassy of Norway Nairobi

Haug, Marie Pedersen, First Secretary Somalia,
Embassy of Denmark Nairobi

Nash, Richard, Governance Adviser, DFID
Nairobi

Nishida, Wataru, General Affairs/Political
Section, Embassy of Japan

Schafer, Leslie, Governance Team Leader,
USAID Nairobi

Schmidt, Anna, European Commission

Sköld, Pär, First Secretary and Senior
Programme Manager of Somalia Section,
Embassy of Sweden Nairobi

Sjöström, Urban, Counsellor and Head of
Development Cooperation of Somalia
Section, Embassy of Sweden Nairobi

Wetugi, Lydia, Embassy of Sweden (Programme
Manager)

Yoshida, Yuki, Researcher/Adviser, Economic
Cooperation Division, Embassy of Japan

Bose, Shipra, Gender Adviser to the Resident
Coordinator

Foschiato, Paola, UN-Women

Maguwi, Pauline, UN-Women

Negrao, Sarah, UNSOM (Senior Gender
Adviser)

Odiit, Martin, Country Director Somalia,
UNAIDS

Vakarelska, Diana, Community Development
Specialist, UNICEF

Van Aaken, Rudi, Head of Office a.i., FAO

Jacquand, Marc, Head, Risk Management Unit,
United Nations in Somalia

MOGADISHU DEVELOPMENT PARTNERS

UNSOM

Matthew, Manoj, Senior Political Affairs Officer
of Political and Mediation Group, UNSOM

Obiorah, Ndubisi, Political Affairs Officer and
Consultation Focal Point of Political and
Mediation Group, UNSOM

Tekinbas, Muustafa, United Nations Police
Commissioner, UNSOM

UNICEF

Delmotte, Jean-Michel, Chief of Field Office
for Mogadishu, Somalia, UNICEF

Matovu, Victoria, Monitoring and Evaluation
Specialist for Mogadishu, Somalia,
UNICEF

CIVIL SOCIETY

Adle, Abdirashid Ali, Head of International
Cooperation Department, Mogadishu
University

Ahmed, Zahra Mohamed, Somali Women
Development Centre

Ali, Dahir Mohamed, Coalition for Grassroots
Women Organisation

Ali, Fatima Sheikh, Coalition for Grassroots
Women Organisation

Arale, Mohamed Mohamoud, Association of
Somali Women Lawyers

Aser, Da'ud Ali, Mogadishu University

Jimale, Habiba Haji, Chairperson, Association
of Somali Women Lawyers Khalif,
Mohamed Sheikh Ahmed, Coalition for
Grassroots Women Organisation

Malaq, Asha, Police Advisory Committee

Mohamed, Abdikadir Salad, Police Advisory
Committee

Elmi, Yusuf Haji, Police Advisory Committee

Elmi, Ahmed Ali, Police Advisory Committee

Haji, Mohamoud Mohamed, AFGOYE
ALIFOW Women Development
Organisation

Sharif, Abdulkarim Mohamed, Executive
Director, AFGOYE ALIFOW Women
Development Organisation

Sharif, Alkarim Moher AFGOYE ALIFOW
Women Development Organisation

Hassan, Abdullahi Hashi, Federal Government
AIDS Commission

Jimale, Ahmed Mohamed, Federal Government
AIDS Commission

Bakaar, Adeh Abdirizak, Horn of Africa
Organization for Protection of Environment
and Improvement of Livelihoods

Fatah, Halima Abdul, Program Office, Aamin
Voluntary and Relief Organization

Hosh, Abdullahim, Project Manager, Center for
Peace and Democracy

Jimale, Abdullali A., Executive Director,
Brotherly Relief and Development
Organization

Mussa,Mahmat, Horn of Africa Organization
for Protection of Environment and
Improvement of Livelihoods

Ibrahim, Abdihalim, Project and Center
Manager, Somali Youth Development
Network

Wehelye, Abdenur Osman, Director,
Organization for Somali Protection and
Development

Abdi, Hassan SH, Vocational Training Director, Ministry of Youth and Sports

Abdullahi, Dahir Abdi, Director General, Ministry of Youth and Sports Mohamed, Awil, Chief of Staff, Ministry of National Security, Federal Government of Somali

Ainte, Ahmed, Director Aid Coordination Unit, Office of the President

Ali, Khalid Omar, Minister, Ministry of Youth and Sports, Federal Government of Somali

Dirshe, Abdi, Permanent Secretary, Ministry of Planning and International Cooperation

Motahed, Abdulkadir Abukar, Finance and Administration Department Head, Ministry of Youth and Sports

Hassan, Abdullali Hasli, Monitoring and Evaluation Officer, Federal Government AIDS Commission

Jimale, Ahmed Mohamed, Executive Director, Federal Government AIDS Commission

Ibrahim, Hanifer Mohamed, Planning Director, Ministry of Youth and Sports

PARLIAMENTARIANS

Roble, Abdulahi Hassan, Parliamentarian, Federal Parliament of Somalia

Buh, Abducarim H Abdi, Parliamentarian, Federal Parliament of Somalia

Hassan, Mohamed Abdulahi, Parliamentarian, Federal Parliament of Somalia

SOMALILAND SPECIAL ARRANGEMENT DEVELOPMENT PARTNERS

GOVERNMENT

Abdi, Mohamed Musa, Director General, Ministry of Labour and Social Affairs

Aideed, Hussein Ahmed, Minister, Ministry of Justice

Jama, Abdi Ali, Executive Director, Somaliland National HIV/AIDS Commission

Mohamoud, Abdinasir Osman, Director of Planning, House of Representatives

Misan, Amal, Special Adviser to the President on Gender

Shire, Sa'ad Ali, Minster, Ministry of National Planning and Development

Iman, Abdillahi Fadel, Brigadier General, Somaliland Police Commissioner

CIVIL SOCIETY

Adan, Hassan, Advocacy Specialist, Nagaad Network

Farah, Mahmoud Hussein, Dean, College of Law, Hargeisa University

Mohamed, Nafisa Yousuf, Executive Director, Nagaad Network

Odowa, Abdullahi, Director, Observatory of Conflict and Violence Prevention

INTERNATIONAL ORGANIZATIONS

Pradhan-Blach, Rima Das, Special Adviser, Minister of National Planning and Development

Rasmussen, Soren Skou, Head of Office and Programme Coordinator, DANIDA

PUNTLAND DEVELOPMENT PARTNERS

GOVERNMENT (GAROWE)

Abdi, Elmi Hassan, Vice Chief Justice, Supreme Court

Abdi, Ismael Hasi, Alternative Dispute Resolution Mechanism Project Focal Point, Ministry of Justice

Abdulali, Buran, Head of Labour Section, Ministry for Youth, Labor and Sports

Adam, Abdul Aziz, Vice-Minister, Ministry of Security and DDR

Adan, Mohamud Abdinor, Chief Executive Officer, Puntland Highway Authority

Ahmed, Abdirahman Sheikh, Minister, Ministry for Youth, Labor and Sports

Ahmed, Barni Isse, HR Director, Ministry for Youth, Labor and Sports

Ali, Awad Hussein, Director General, Ministry of Security and DDR

Ali, Said Adan, Mayor of Bandar Beyle

Barre, Guled Salah, Minister of Environment, Wildlife and Tourism

Bile, Ahmed Hassan, Director General, Ministry for Youth, Labor and Sports

Dr Jama, Abdisamed Ahmed, Director, Garowe General Hospital

Dr Mahmoud, Abdurahman Said, Executive Director, Puntland AIDS Commission

Elmi, Abdelkadir Nur, Joint Programme on Local Governance, Local Governance Consultant, Ministry of Interior

Fandhaal, Abdifatah, Senior Security Adviser, Ministry of Security and DDR

Fatah, Ali Ahmed, Minister of Planning

Garow, Mohammed Yussuf, Mayor of Hafun

Hajimumin, Anisa, Minister for Women and Family Affairs

Hassan, Osman Mahmoud, Attorney General, Supreme Court

Ismael, Abdurazak Sheir, Deputy Minister, Ministry for Youth, Labor and Sports

Mohamed, Abderizak Nouw, Director General, Minister of Justice

Mohamoud, Abdukadir Ahmed, Chief Justice, Supreme Court

Mohamad, Ahmed Yassin, Coordinator of Community Safety and Peace Building, Ministry of Security and DDR

Mohamed, Mohamed Abdulali, Head of IT Department, Ministry for Youth, Labor and Sports

Mohammed, Said Abdurahman, Mayor of Bosaso

Musa, Abshir Mohamud, Director of Maintenance Department, Puntland Highway Authority

Musa, Mohammed Yusuf, Joint Programme on Local Governance Planning Consultant, Ministry of Interior

Nur, Abdulaziz, Mayor of Garowe

Nur, Mohammed Ali, Director of Planning, Ministry of Interior

Said, Abdullah, Director General, Ministry of Interior

Suleiman, Mohamed Jama, Financial Officer, Minister of Justice

Warsame, Abdullah Hashi, Deputy Minister, Ministry of Interior

Warsame, Ali Mohamed, Administration and Finance Officer, Minister of Justice

Warsame, Mohamed Bashir, Program Officer, Minister of Justice

Warsame, Ismael Mohamed, Minister of Justice

Warsame, Said, Commander, Special Police Unit

Yussuf, Musa Osman, Mayor of Eyl

CIVIL SOCIETY (GAROWE)

Aadan, Caisho Abshir, Relief and Development Centre

Abdulahi, Fatima, Vice-chair, Puntland Women Lawyers Association

Ali, Abdimalik Osman, Relief and Development Centre

Ali, Abdurachid, Manager, Somali Family Services

Ali, Fathi Harsi, Chairperson, Puntland Women Lawyers Association

Atcyc, Samsan Ali, Forum for Africa Women Educationist, Somalia

Egol, Yurab Hersi, Forum for Africa Women Educationist, Somalia

Elmi, Faisu Abdulahi, member, Puntland Women Lawyers Association

Farah, Farah Mohamed, General Secretary, Puntland Environmental Protection Association

Hassan, Suleiqa, Timely Integrated Development Services

Hassan, Abdirahim, Timely Integrated Development Services

Husain, Ahmad Isse, Field Coordinator, Puntland Center for Human Rights and Demography

Hussein, Saada Abdi, Gender Adviser, SAMOFAL (NGO)

Jama, Hamdi Abshin, Secretary, Puntland Women Lawyers Association

Jama, Sucdi Mohamed, Relief and Development Centre

Ibrahim, Ahmed, Administrative Officer, Direct Aid and Nature Development Organisation

Nuur, Fadumo Diiriye, Executive Director, SAMOFAL (NGO)

Nuur, Yusuf Haji, Puntland Legal Centre

Omar, Burhan Adan, Director , Legal Aid Clinic, Puntland

Said, Mahamoud Mohammed, Relief and Development Centre

Yusuf, Nasro Dahir, Relief and Development Centre

GOVERNMENT (GARDO)

Ali, Said Barre, Gardo Prison Commander

Mohamed, Mohamed Abdulaziz, Director, Development and Planning Department, Gardo District

Shire, Mahamoud Mohamed, Executive Director, Gardo District Administration

CIVIL SOCIETY (GARDO)

Ahmed, Abdirashid, Project Manager, Puntland Development Organisation

Ali, Mohamed, Site Supervisor, Puntland Development Organisation

Ibrahim, Amir, Admin and Finance Officer, Puntland Development Organisation

Isak, Sakiraya, Office Manager, Puntland Development Organisation

Yasin, Abdi Kadir, Chairman, Puntland Development Organisation

LIST OF PROJECTS

PUNTLAND

1. Galkayo Vocational Training Centre
2. Bosaso Market
3. Empowering Women of Eyl and Improving their Resilience
4. Galkayo Peace Market
5. Rehabilitation of Dawad-Badey Road in Eyl District
6. Youth for Change (Y4C) and Eyl Business Services Development Centre
7. Rehabilitation of Irrigation Water Canals and Construction of Water Tank
8. BADBAADO Community Conversations on HIV/AIDS
9. Galkayo Educational Centre for Peace and Development

SOMALILAND

1. Construction of Burao Deaf School
2. Burao Hospital Solar Energy System
3. Community Conversations on HIV/AIDS
4. Partial Rehabilitation and Operationalization of Burao Technical Institute
5. Prosecutor's Regional Office in Burao
6. Joint Programme for Local Governance - Berbera Municipality,
7. Baahikoob Center
8. Somaliland Women's Lawyers Association
9. Berbera Fish Project
10. Hargeisa Legal Aid Clinic
11. Hargeisa Community Model Police Station
12. Construction of Sheikh Bashir Primary School

FEDERAL GOVERNMENT

1. Provision of Vocational Skills Training and Micro Grants Project, Adado (Galgaduud)
2. Construction of New Market Facility and Extension of Existing Market Facilities in Adado District (Galgaduud Region)
3. The Political and Civic Empowerment of Women in Galgaduud Region
4. Youth for Change – Resource Centers for Peace in Wadajir, Hamar Jajab and Kaaran Districts

DOCUMENTS CONSULTED

COUNTRY BACKGROUND

African Development Bank (AFDB), Organisation for Economic Cooperation and Development (OECD) and UNDP, 'African Economic Outlook', Somalia, 2014.

AFDB, 'Somalia Country Brief for 2013-2015', 2013.

European Commission, 'Gender Audit of the EC Somalia Mission Final Report', October 2013.

FAO Evaluation Office, 'Evaluation of FAO's Cooperation in Somalia, 2007 to 2012', 2014.

Federal Republic of Somalia, 'Provisional Constitution', Mogadishu, August 1, 2012.

Federal Republic of Somalia, 'The Somali Compact', Brussels, September 2013.

Galli F. and Riverson J. et al., 'Somali Joint Needs Assessment - Infrastructure Cluster Report', World Bank, September 2006.

Hammond L., Awad M., Dagane A., Hansen P., Horst C., Menkhaus K. and Obare L., 'Cash and Compassion: The Role of the Somali Diaspora in Relief, Development and Peacebuilding', UNDP Somalia, January 2011.

Hussein A., 'Institutionalizing Islamic Finance in South Central Somalia', UNDP Somalia, March 2013.

LOGICA, 'Gender and Conflict Note', Somalia, March 2013.

Menkhaus, K., 'Conflict Analysis: Somalia' paper prepared for UNSOM', 2014 (draft).

Mohamed A., 'Final Report on Youth for Change Project (December 2012 - October 2013)', Capital Administration of Puntland State of Somalia and Ministry of Security and DDR, Garowe, 2014.

Puntland Highway Authority (PHA), 'Final Reports on Jariban-Galkacyo Road Project and on Eyl Road Project', Garowe, December 2013.

Sarah P., 'Political Settlements and State Formation: The Case of Somaliland', Development leadership Programme Research Paper 23, December 2013.

Transitional Federal Government, '2010 Millennium Development Goals Progress Report for Somalia', Mogadishu, 2010.

UNDP Somalia, 'Gender in Somalia Brief', Gender Unit, undated.

UNDP Somalia, 'Somalia Human Development Report 2012 - Empowering Youth for Peace and Development', 2012.

UNDP Somalia, 'Islamic Microfinance Workshop Report', Khartoum, 11–13 March 2013.

UNDP Somalia, 'Somalia and the Enhanced Integrated Framework (EIF)', April 2014.

United Nations, 'Report of the Monitoring Group on Somalia and Eritrea pursuant to Security Council resolution 2060 (2012): Eritrea', S/2013/413, 25 July 2013.

USAID Somalia, 'Environmental and Natural Resource Management Assessment', April 2014.

USAID Somalia, 'Gender Assessment-Navigating Gender Roles and Status to Benefit Men and Women Equally', 2014.

Women in Development (IIDA), 'Policy brief on constitution', http://allafrica.com/stories/201210310067.html.

Somalia Water and Land Information Management (SWALIM), Update Quarterly Newsletter, May - July 2013, Issue 2: SWALIM Locates Source of the Kismayo Charcoal Pile.

EVALUATIONS

Abbott K., Palmbach M. and Rao P., 'External Evaluation of Somali Institutional Development Project', UNDP Somalia, May 2014.

ADA Consultants Inc., 'Employment generation for Early Recovery Project (EGER) and Area Based Early Recovery Project (ABER) Evaluation Report', Quebec, Canada, 2013.

Adam Smith International, 'Evaluation of the UNDP Strategic Partnership for Somalia', 2009.

BBC Media Action, 'UNDP Somalia HIV and AIDS Media Project. Impact Evaluation Research Report', 2012.

Bonard P. and Conoir Y., 'Evaluation of UNDP Reintegration Programs: Somaliland Case Study', UNDP BCPR, New York, 2013.

Donnelly P. and Bugembe J., 'Final Evaluation: UN Joint Programme on Local Governance and Decentralised Service Delivery', Phase 1, UNDP Somalia, Nairobi, 2014.

Eavis P., Hills A., McLean A. and Mennen T., 'Evaluation of ROLS III Programme', UNDP Somalia, 2011.

Guillemois D., Mohamed M. S. and Mohamed M. I., 'Evaluation of the "Youth at Risk project" and some security related components', Final Report, UNDP Somalia, December 2012.

Intermedia Development Consultants, 'Joint Programme for Local Governance, Evaluation report', 2013.

Norad, 'Review of the Norwegian Support to Somalia though UNDP', Norad Report 10/2013, Oslo, Norway, 2013.

Rispo M., 'Evaluation of UNDP supported mobile courts interventions in Somaliland, Sierra Leone and Democratic Republic of Congo-Somaliland County Study', UNDP BCPR, New York, 2013.

Thery A. and Amici A., 'Evaluation of the UNDP Somali Institutional Development Programme', UNDP Somalia, February 2012.

UNDP Evaluation Office, 'Assessment of Development Results Somalia', 2010.

UNDP Evaluation Office and Katuni Consult, 'Beneficiary Assessment Report Draft Report for Somaliland', 2014.

NATIONAL PLANNING DOCUMENTS

The Federal Republic of Somalia, 'The Somali Compact', Mogadishu, 2013.

Puntland State of Somalia, 'Puntland Second Five-Year Development Plan, 2014 - 2018, Development For All', Garowe, 2013.

Puntland State of Somalia, 'Five Year Development Strategy, 2012-2016', Garowe, 2011.

UNDP PROGRAMMING DOCUMENTS

UNDP Somalia, 'Country Programme Document', 2011-2015.

UNDP Somalia, 'Framework for Private Sector Development in Somalia', 2013.

UNDP Somalia, 'Gender Equality and Women's Empowerment Strategy (2011 – 2015)', 21 Jan 2014.

UNDP Somalia, 'Gender Equality and Women's Empowerment Strategy (2011-2015) Progress Report', 2012 and 2013.

UNDP Somalia, 'Poverty reduction and environmental protection Project Document', 2011.

UNDP Somalia, 'Programme Document - Strengthening Gender Equality and Women's Empowerment in Somalia,' (2012-2015).

UNDP Somalia, 'Somalia Gender Equality Annual Report', 2012 and 2013.

UNDP REPORTING DOCUMENTS

UNDP, 'Gender Equality Seal, Assessment Report', 2014.

UNDP, 'Gender Parity Strategy', 2012.

UNDP, 'Gender Mainstreaming Made Easy, Handbook for Programme Staff', 2013.

UNDP Somalia, 'Annual Report', 2011, 2012, 2013.

UNDP Somalia, 'Annual Project Reports' (Various), 2011, 2012, 2013.

UNDP Somalia, 'Gender in Somalia, Brief', 2014.

UNDP Somalia, 'Project Annual and Quarterly Reports for LED, Environment Project, Community Security Project', 2011, 2012, 2013.

UNDP Somalia, 'Results Oriented Annual Report', 2011, 2012, 2013.

UNDP Somalia, 'Resident Coordinator Annual Report', 2011, 2012, 2013.

UNDP Somalia, 'Somalia Human Development Report: Empowering Youth for Peace and Development', 2012.

UNDP Somalia, 'The Role of Somalia Women in Private Sector', 2014.

UNDP, United Nations Office for Project Services and UN-Women, 'Violence in the lives of Girls and Women in Somalia', 2012.

UNFPA, 'Female Genital Mutilation/Cutting: Accelerating Change', 2012.

United Nations, 'Report of the Secretary-General on Somalia', March 2014.

MANAGEMENT RESPONSE

<table>
<tr><td colspan="6">Evaluation recommendation 1. Recognizing the complexity and fluidity of the Somali context, the ADR recommends that UNDP Somalia, in developing its new country programme, should continue to pursue an adaptive planning and management approach.

The validity of medium- to long-term planning approaches in a high-risk environment characterized by rapidly changing political, security and humanitarian situations such as Somalia's merits closer examination. The planning and management of the programme, including decisions on staff relocation, should remain flexible enough to allow for progressive elaboration of strategies and short-term results and targets based on newly emerging developments. This approach will minimize potential retrofitting of predetermined priorities under emergent frameworks, as seen under the current country programme when a new Government and new aid architecture materialized in 2012 and 2013. Somalia will be holding elections and developing a national development plan in 2016. The country office should use the best available expertise and technical support from within and outside UNDP to design a new country programme that is adaptable to changing conditions and balances between Somalia' short-term and long-term development needs.</td></tr>
<tr><td colspan="6">Management response

UNDP Somalia agrees with this recommendation. UNDP has maintained its flexibility in the Somali context by: (a) aligning its programmes to the New Deal priorities and the Compact's peacebuilding and State-building goals and by designing and aligning new programmes under the Compact aid architecture; (b) expanding its portfolio specifically to support key political priorities, including electoral support, review of the Constitution and support to newly emerging federal member states, focusing on both the short-term political deliverables and on building institutional capacity for longer term democratic development in Somalia; (c) expanding its institutional support to governance institutions such as parliaments in the newly emerging federal member states; and (d) developing a comprehensive youth employment strategy and joint programme to support the long-term employability of Somali youth through strengthening of value chains in key growth sectors, and rolling out new programming to support climate change resilience at community level.

UNDP Somalia is currently supporting the Federal Government in preparing its first National Development Plan (NDP) in more than two decades, in order to focus future development interventions on poverty reduction and address the root causes of vulnerability that underlie the volatile humanitarian context, while continuing to maintain an integrated focus on the intersection between politics, security and development. UNDP will develop its next country programme in alignment with the NDP. The future country programme will reiterate the need for flexibility with regard to immediate priorities while maintaining a commitment to longer-term development objective and the Sustainable Development Goals.</td></tr>
<tr><td rowspan="2">Key Action(s)</td><td rowspan="2">Time Frame</td><td rowspan="2">Responsible Unit(s)</td><td colspan="2">Tracking*</td></tr>
<tr><td>Status</td><td>Comments</td></tr>
<tr><td>Development of new CPD in alignment with the Government's new National Development Plan (NDP)</td><td>2016-2017</td><td>PPU</td><td></td><td></td></tr>
</table>

Management response.

The country office is in broad agreement with the recommendation. The country office's programmatic portfolio on poverty reduction and resilience has been expanding rapidly. Key new projects include the Joint Programme on Youth Employment Somalia (2015–2018), with UN-Habitat, ILO and FAO; the Joint Programme for Sustainable Charcoal Reduction and Alternative Livelihoods, with FAO and UNEP; and the Enhancing Climate Resilience of the Vulnerable Communities and Ecosystems in Somalia (2015-2018), funded by the Global Environment Facility. The country office is also developing a new joint programme on durable solutions to displacement in Somalia, with UN-Habitat and UNHCR, as well as new initiatives related to renewable energy, climate-smart approaches to rural development and local economic development.

However, the country office recognizes the need for a forward-looking review of the poverty reduction and environment programme with a focus on longer-term poverty reduction, including shifting from short-term employment to longer-term employment at scale, particularly for youth and women, that will drive economic growth and support overall stability. The new NDP will provide a key opportunity for UNDP to reposition its work – and its engagement with the Government and donor partners – in favour of a greater focus on poverty reduction, and a strategic review as suggested would likewise assist in this respect.

The comments on regular resources are well noted. regular resources have played a critical role in initiating new programmes, and in bridging gaps when donor funding is sometimes unpredictable. A flexible approach to TRAC allocations is thereby necessary.

Key Action(s)	Time Frame	Responsible Unit(s)	Tracking*	
			Status	Comments
Forward-looking review of the poverty reduction and environment programme	Q4 2016	PPU		

Management response

The country office is in broad agreement with the recommendation. The findings of the ADR concerning the often limited impact of capacity development efforts were recognized and led to the development of a new capacity development programme during 2014 and the beginning of 2015, consisting of two main projects: strengthening institutional performance, working on the federal level and in Puntland; and the state formation project, working in the emerging states. Both projects became, operational during 2015. These are in addition to longstanding support to district governments through the joint programme on local governance, which is now being expanded to new districts in the south of the country.

Improvements in the country office's overall approach to capacity development are taking place on three levels:

- **Focusing capacity development towards core government functions**, including planning, monitoring, evaluation and statistics; organizational structures and functional arrangements on vertical and horizontal levels; internal and external coordination mechanisms; civil service management, with a strong focus on human resource management; administrative management (including financial, personnel, office systems, etc.); policy and strategy development (systemic improvements); and gender mainstreaming in selected key areas;

- **Focusing capacity development support on the internal capacities of supporting institutions**, in line with the overall UNDP approach to capacity development, with its focus on organizational development, and directly linked to the HACT capacity assessments and functional reviews undertaken. The support provided to government institutions focuses on strengthening internal systems of governance as well as the individual capacities of staff members to discharge their functions; organizational reforms; regulatory development; designing terms of reference; and classic training of the supporting institutions' staff;

- **Stimulating consistency in the capacity development approach throughout the country programme.** While specific capacity development projects are being delivered at federal, state and district levels, as noted above, capacity development is an important and cross-cutting element of all UNDP-supported projects. Steps have been taken to further harmonize the capacity development approach and stimulate a higher level of coherence in the country programme. This element, however, does require more attention, and will be taken forward through the formulation of the new country programme. which is likely to occur toward the end of 2016, bringing the overall programme structure in line with the expectations of the forthcoming NDP.

Key Action(s)	Time Frame	Responsible Unit(s)	Tracking*	
			Status	Comments
Implementation of capacity development approach for national partners, including: - Internal guidance on HACT capacity assessments and functional reviews - Improved framework for management of letters of agreement. - Initial set of role and responsibility distribution between federal, state and district level governments, to guide capacity development initiatives. - Federal-, state- and district-level training strategies.	2016-2017	PPU, CD Unit, Governance Unit.		

Management response

UNDP Somalia agrees with this recommendation. The CPD for 2011-2016 had a dedicated gender-specific outcome and provided a framework within which to implement the corporate mandate of gender mainstreaming across all country programme outcomes. The country office has made efforts and progress in consolidating past gains, building on lessons learned and drawing inspiration from corporate commitments to gender equality and women's empowerment, as reflected in the Gender Equality Seal High Silver award which the country office received in 2015. Recommendations from the Gender Equality Seal process are now being implemented, in order to progress towards a target of Gold. The country office, together with other UNCT members, has supported gender representation in the Somali Compact processes, including two side-events on women and gender equity issues at the High-Level Partnership Forums in 2015 and 2016. To attain even further results in terms of gender mainstreaming, the country office will focus on the following:

a) Mainstreaming gender empowerment and women's empowerment in the next country programme;

b) Continued delivery of specific initiatives to advance gender empowerment and women's empowerment, including on women's political participation, the gender dimension of the National Development Plan and Sustainable Development Goal 5;

c) Building and strengthening strategic partnerships to increase the impact of efforts to promote gender empowerment and women's empowerment , as recommended by the ADR;

d) Improving gender-responsive planning, monitoring, reporting and evaluation.

Key Action(s)	Time Frame	Responsible Unit(s)	Tracking*	
			Status	Comments
Inclusion of one outcome on gender equality and women's empowerment in new CPD and continued delivery of specific initiatives to advance gender equality and women's empowerment	2016-2017	PPU and Cross-Cutting unit (CCU)		
Capacity-building of key partners to increase impact on gender equality and women's empowerment, including through the review of financial allocations in project planning documents and mainstreaming gender in implementing partner agreements	2016-2017	CCU		
Gender-responsive project monitoring, reporting and evaluation framework	Q4 2016	CCU, PPU		

Evaluation recommendation 5. UNDP should increase investments to enhance internal monitoring and reporting capacities. It is encouraging that UNDP has already initiated alternative institutional arrangements to strengthen results-based monitoring and reporting, such as third-party monitoring in 2015. Capacities of implementing partners to monitor their work during implementation and ex-post should also be assessed and strengthened as part of broader capacity development efforts.

Given that the ability of UNDP Somalia staff to monitor programme implementation is curtailed by insecurity, inaccessibility and other constraints, the engagement by UNDP of an institution for third-party monitoring in early 2015 is a positive step. The office is also cognizant that the focus of such monitoring must move away from mere numbers and attempt to highlight the contribution of UNDP to intermediate results.

UNDP should continue to identify internal learning needs in relation to results-based monitoring and reporting. Repeated training opportunities including both formal training and on-the-job orientation are needed since one-off results-based management training is not sufficient to improve skills. Strengthening nascent national monitoring and reporting capacities is also relevant as the country prepares its post Vision 2016 national development framework. Some of these efforts can build on ongoing initiatives such as the rolling out the HACT and must move away from being compliance-based capacity development.

Management response

UNDP Somalia agrees with this recommendation. The country office has strengthened internal monitoring and reporting through a number of means, including increasing the number of national M&E staff in projects and in the Programme and Planning Unit. The third-party monitoring arrangements in place not only verify numbers or activities, but also seeks more output- and outcome-related results, including beneficiary satisfaction and project effectiveness, among others. All project documents, annual workplans and partnership agreements are reviewed by the M&E team prior to approval. Similarly, all implementation arrangements (letters of agreement, grants, etc.) are scrutinized through the Local Project Appraisal Committee, to ensure that proper capacity assessment and appropriate risk mitigation measures have been put in place. The letters of agreement and grant agreements also contain requirements for improved partner reporting, third-party monitoring as commissioned by UNDP and provision of beneficiary contacts in order to conduct follow up verification. The office has revised its reporting templates with a focus on evidence-based reporting and inclusion of monitoring and oversight activities.

In 2016, the country office will continue to develop these arrangements. Work is ongoing to deepen capacity development of national counterparts specifically in the areas of results- based management and reporting. This includes specific support, for instance, to the new M&E team at the Ministry of Planning and International cooperation on results-based management and monitoring of progress towards the Sustainable Development Goals, and on the preparation of the monitoring framework for the new NDP. The country office will continue these efforts through devising a feedback mechanism for senior management on monitoring findings and follow-up actions; expanded capacity development of national partners on results-based management and reporting; establishment of a country office M&E working group for national staff; tracking frequency of monitoring visits undertaken by project and programme staff; and using social media inform stakeholders of third-party monitoring findings.

Key Action(s)	Time Frame	Responsible Unit(s)	Tracking*	
			Status	Comments
Capacity development plan of national implementing partners on monitoring and reporting	2016-2017	PPU		
Establishment of CO Monitoring and Evaluation Working Group	2016	PPU		
Establishment of management feedback mechanism on TPM	2016	PPU		
Development and usage of a compliance tracking tool for project and programme staff monitoring activities	2016	PPU		
Development of a communication strategy/approach to disseminate TPM findings through social media	2016-17	PPU		

* The implementation status is tracked in the UNDP Evaluation Resource Centre.